Childhood in Kinship Care

Kinship foster care involves placing children who cannot live at home in foster care with other members of their family or close network. This book sheds light on different aspects of kinship care development and practice.

Using a 20-year longitudinal research study from Norway, this book shows the historical development of kinship care in Norway, research on kinship care and how family life and relations are negotiated and lived in the span between private and public sphere. It includes the perspectives of the children, their parents and their relatives who have functioned as foster parents. Recognising that kinship care is complex, and needs to be understood and studied from different perspectives, the book describes, analyses and discusses a number of subjects: kinship care in a child welfare historical context, families who are part of kinship care and their perspectives, the formal frameworks around kinship care and research approaches which have dominated research into kinship care.

This book will be of interest to all scholars, students and professionals working in social work and child welfare more broadly, both in the Nordic countries and in a wider international context.

Jeanette Skoglund is associate professor at RKBU North, Faculty of Health Sciences, UiT The Arctic University of Norway.

Renee Thørnblad is professor RKBU North, Faculty of Health Sciences, UiT The Arctic University of Norway.

Amy Holtan is professor emerita at RKBU North, Faculty of Health Sciences, UiT The Arctic University of Norway.

Childhood in Kinship Care
A Longitudinal Investigation

Jeanette Skoglund,
Renee Thørnblad and
Amy Holtan

Routledge
Taylor & Francis Group
LONDON AND NEW YORK

First published 2022
by Routledge
4 Park Square, Milton Park, Abingdon, Oxon OX14 4RN

and by Routledge
605 Third Avenue, New York, NY 10158

Routledge is an imprint of the Taylor & Francis Group, an informa business

© 2022 Jeanette Skoglund, Renee Thørnblad and Amy Holtan

The right of Jeanette Skoglund, Renee Thørnblad and Amy Holtan to be identified as authors of this work has been asserted in accordance with sections 77 and 78 of the Copyright, Designs and Patents Act 1988.

Trademark notice: Product or corporate names may be trademarks or registered trademarks, and are used only for identification and explanation without intent to infringe.

British Library Cataloguing-in-Publication Data
A catalogue record for this book is available from the British Library

Library of Congress Cataloging-in-Publication Data
A catalog record has been requested for this book

ISBN: 978-1-032-13889-3 (hbk)
ISBN: 978-1-032-13894-7 (pbk)
ISBN: 978-1-003-23136-3 (ebk)

DOI: 10.4324/9781003231363

Typeset in Times New Roman
by codeMantra

Contents

Figures

Tables

Preface

The book springs from more than 20 years of research into kinship
care. We have followed the development of kinship care as a research
field in Norway, in the other Nordic countries and internationally from
a time when social workers were critical to foster care in the child's
family to the present, when kinship care is an integrated social policy,
prioritised by CWS.

The book is the first of its kind in the Nordic countries. Our aim is to
make visible the complexity behind the phenomenon, that is, kinship
care. We want to challenge the frameworks of the conceptual understandings of the CWS, and with the help of sociological theory discuss
different aspects of growing up in foster care among one's own kin.
Kinship care families practise their family life in the intersection of
the private and the public sphere. The signing of a foster care agreement between the CWS and the child's relatives widens the scope and
extent of official authority. Child welfare cases are not only about the
children and their parents, but also about aunts, uncles, grandparents
or other relatives who assume the responsibility of caring for the child.
Kinship care can be understood in two ways: both as a child welfare
intervention and as family, of which there is diversity of types in our
society today.

The book is a result of a research project on kinship care which over
a period has resulted in three doctoral theses. When the project was
initiated it was innovative for several reasons: the subject was a scantly
investigated field, children and young people were involved as informants, and it had a longitudinal design. Over the years we interviewed
the children when they were in primary school, as teenagers and as
young adults. The data have provided scope for both qualitative and
quantitative analysis.

We would like to say a warm thank you to all the participants in our
research project who have allowed us to interview them and who have

filled in questionnaires over an extended period. It would not have been possible to write this book without their shared experiences.

We would also like to thank the Regional Centre for Child and Youth Mental Health and Child Welfare, RKBU North, who have funded our research project and the publication of this book. Lastly, we want to thank Routledge and the book's translator Kirsti Spaven for an excellent collaboration.

Jeanette Skoglund,
Renee Thørnblad and Amy Holtan

1 Introduction

Kinship care as a professionalised, priority child welfare intervention

Through the ages relatives have often taken care of children who for various reasons could not be looked after by their parents and who therefore needed a home. *Kinship foster care,* on the other hand, as an intervention and category in the child welfare services (CWS), is a relatively new phenomenon. There are several terms for growing up in foster care with relatives, both nationally and internationally. In Sweden, kinship foster care is known as *släktinghem* ('kinship home'), in Denmark as *slægtspleje* ('family care'), and in Norway as *slektsfosterhjem* ('kinship foster care') and *fosterhjem i familie og nettverk* (foster care in family and network). In English-speaking countries, such as the USA, the UK and Australia, it is known as *kinship foster care, family and friends care* and *kith and kin care.* In this book, kinship care will refer to kinship foster care placements, and non-kinship care will refer to traditional foster care placements.

The understanding of the suitability of relatives as foster parents in CWS has changed over time. With the growth of the welfare states and the entry of various professions into the field of child welfare, especially from the 1970s, interventions and services for children who were unable to grow up with their birth parents became professionalised. This emerging specialisation of child welfare resulted in relatives frequently being regarded as inadequate caregivers for such children (Moldestad, 1996; Vinnerljung, 1996; Winokur, Holtan, & Valentine, 2009). In the Nordic countries however, as well as in other Western countries (Winokur, Holtan, & Batchelder, 2014; Sundt, 2012) there has been a change in this respect, and relatives have gradually gained a more positive status in the professional child welfare field. In Norway, new regulations on foster care came into force in 2004, marking a turning point in governmental attitudes and policy towards relatives as

DOI: 10.4324/9781003231363-1

foster parents. Section 4 of the regulations states that "the child welfare services shall always consider whether someone in the child's family or immediate network can be chosen as a foster home". In 2018, the duty of municipal authorities to look for a foster home in the child's family and immediate network was included in the Child Welfare Act (Section 4–22). At the end of 2020, 3,239 children and young people aged 0–22 lived in kinship and close network foster care in Norway. That constituted 32.5 percent of all children in foster homes (SSB, 2021).[1]

The inclusion of kinship care in CWS may be seen as an expansion of the field of child welfare. When a foster family is formalised in this way, the children are ascribed client status in the services and their caregivers are defined as foster parents. The family members become subject to official approval, financing and control in line with non-kinship foster families. As a child welfare intervention, *kinship care* follows the terminology, procedures and legal authority of the CWS. In practical terms, however, the criteria used by the CWS are to some extent different when approving kinship care, in that the importance of relationships may compensate for qualities which normally are more strongly emphasised in the approval of non-kinship foster homes.

Why a book on kinship care?

The institutionalisation and prioritisation of kinship care as an intervention implies an increased need for knowledge about the phenomenon, for decision-makers at various levels, practitioners, researchers and others working directly or indirectly with kinship care. Only a few decades ago, kinship placement was an unexplored research field. Not until the early 1990s did kinship care appear as a research topic, initially in the USA. Research contributions from the Nordic countries were few in this period.

Faced with this lack of knowledge, Amy Holtan embarked on her doctoral research on kinship care in 1998. Her interest in the topic stemmed from her time as an expert member on the county social welfare board, where, when dealing with a case, she was confronted with her own attitude, as well as that of the CWS, of preferring to avoid foster placements within the child's own family. The case in question resulted in the children's services ruling against kinship placement, giving very generalised reasons for their decision. In the preface of her doctoral thesis (2002) she wrote:

> It was not clear what the child welfare services had based their decision on, and the woman's [the grandmother's] proposal was not followed up with a thorough investigation by the child welfare services. I began to search the literature in order to find out whether

the practice of the child welfare services had a base in research. I could find no such documentation. I therefore want to investigate the field further, in order to acquire research-based knowledge on kinship foster care.

What began as a single study (1998–2002) on the social integration of children in kinship care was later extended to become a research project with the aim of following up the same children, their parents and grandparents over time. The research project, also known as "Outcomes and Experience of Foster Care",[2] has resulted in a further two doctoral theses, carried out by the other two authors of this book: Renee Thørnblad (2011) and Jeanette Skoglund (2018).

During the course of the 20 years of the project we have published a number of scientific research articles on various aspects of kinship care in both national and international journals. Some other Norwegian, Swedish and Danish researchers also contributed to the acquisition of knowledge during this period. Kinship care is, in other words, no longer an uninvestigated topic in the Nordic countries. This Nordic research is, however, largely inaccessible to the English-speaking world, and for that reason we decided to have our book translated into English. The book was originally published in Norwegian in 2020, when it was the first textbook to deal with kinship care in the Nordic countries. The book is based on our doctoral theses and scientific articles, but here they have been further developed.

Objectives and theoretical frameworks

The aim of this book is to shine a light on kinship care as a phenomenon. An important starting point is that kinship care is complex and needs to be understood and studied from different perspectives in order to gain a deeper understanding of this phenomenon and what it involves. In the book we do it by describing, analysing and discussing a number of subjects: kinship care in a child welfare historical context, the families who are part of kinship care and the perspectives of the involved parties, the formal frameworks within which kinship care is practised and the research approaches which have dominated research into kinship care. Theoretical perspectives are important, not only to explain social circumstances or understand contexts, but also to explore and understand kinship care in new ways.

A large proportion of the kinship care research is based on theory from psychology and social work. The theoretical perspectives we use in the book are taken from social science in general and sociology in particular. The sociological contributions we draw on range from theoretical ideas developed to explain how we can understand contemporary society, to concepts illustrating contemporary family life, parenthood and relationships. Altogether, these various theoretical contributions constitute our tools for describing, investigating and discussing kinship care and the social reality in which the phenomenon exists.

The book is written for students and professions of child welfare and social work, both in the Nordic countries and in a wider international context. The book also has relevance beyond the field of child welfare, since research on kinship care touches on areas such as childhood, kinship, family, parenthood and welfare in general. This makes the book relevant also for social scientists and others working in the fields of family and family welfare.

Data from three time points

The data we use in this book are taken from our research project "Outcomes and Experience of Foster Care", a national study with a longitudinal design.[3] Data for the original selection were collected for the first time in 1999/2000 (T1) and consisted of a group of children aged between 4 and 12 (born between 1986 and 1995). The children were in the custody of the CWS and had lived in foster homes (kinship care and non-kinship care) for a minimum of one year. The second data collection was carried out in 2007/2008 (T2). The children had grown up into teenagers and young adults. The final data collection was carried out in 2014/2015, when the "children" were between 19 and 29 years old (see Table 1.1). The research project is one of two in the Nordic countries which study the experiences and impact of kinship care over time.[4]

Table 1.1 Research project data from three studies

The research project "Outcomes and Experience of Foster Care"									
Informants	*T1 1999/2000*			*T2 2006/2008*			*T3 2014/2015*	
	CBCL/ PSI[5]	*Survey*	*Interview*	*CBCL/ ASR*	*Survey*	*Interview*	*Survey*	*Interview*
Children			X	X	X	X	X	X
Birth parents			X					
Foster parents	X	X	X	X	X			

Today we take the need for research using children and young people as informants for granted. However, when this project was at the planning stage towards the end of the 1990s, children were rarely used as informants in child welfare research. There were vociferous opinions, including among sociologists, that children should be protected and that interviewing them might be too much of a burden. Until the end of the 1990s, the sources of child welfare research and research into children in foster care had in the main been represented by adults. A report on child welfare research, 1997–2001, emphasised the following:

> It seems natural that a renewed research effort to a greater extent is directed towards the experiences and perspectives of clients, and how the services of the welfare state through the child welfare services actually work for people who are affected by the law.
>
> (The Research Council of Norway, 1997)

Our project originates from this period. The task was to study the social integration of children, with particular emphasis on the child's experience of family and belonging. The project was based on the understanding that an official care order is an intervention of great significance in the life of disadvantaged children and their families. As mentioned above, very little research on kinship care, and with children as informants, had been carried out in the Nordic countries. The children therefore became the primary interview objects throughout the whole study. We followed them at three time points, until the oldest were approaching the age of 30. Other informants were foster parents and birth parents. The study had two samples, children in kinship and non-kinship foster homes.

Characteristics of the Kinship families in the research project

The four major characteristics of the kinship foster families in our project are set out below. These provide some guide rails for the book:

• **In foster homes with relatives**: All the children grew up in foster homes with relatives, that is, grandparents, uncles, aunts or other family members. This clarification is important, because the formal definition of kinship care in Norway also includes networks. Network can be defined as relative stable social relations such as friends, teachers and neighbours. Since network relationships are not represented in our study, the topic is not included in the book.

• **Self-recruited**: A large number of the families were self-recruited, meaning that the family members themselves took the initiative to care for a particular child, rather than signal a general interest in becoming foster parents. Of the families in our selection, only one in five children (19 percent) had been placed in kinship care following an initiative from the CWS (Holtan, 2002). Many children were already living with their relatives *before* the foster care formalisation. Kinship care in this book is, in other words, to a large extent about children who had established relationships with their foster parents before an agreement of foster care was entered into.

• **Formal kinship care**: Internationally there are several variations of kinship care, including *formal, informal* and *private placements* (Winokur et al., 2014, p. 3). All the families who took part in our research project were part of formal kinship care placements, meaning that they were legal arrangements where the child was in the custody of the CWS. Private kinship care, on the other hand, refers to voluntary arrangements between birth parents and relatives without the involvement of the CWS. In informal kinship care placements, CWS assist in the placement but do not seek custody. Unlike in other countries, private or informal kinship care placements are not relevant categories in Norwegian kinship care research.[6]

• **Children in the custody of the state**: All the children were in the custody of the state. That is to say they were not living in kinship care as a relief measure, as some children do. This can influence how the arrangement works in practice. In relief measure arrangements, the children's birth parents retain the formal care. In our sample of cases, custody of the child was removed from the parents and legally transferred to the CWS.

The terminology of the child welfare services

CWS in Norway and other countries use a comprehensive terminology in order to classify and describe children and young people who grow up in the custody of the state and the interventions that are put in place. Concepts such as "foster child", "foster parents", "homes as foster homes", "placement", "visitation" and "after care" are examples of this. According to Andenæs (2011, p. 487), the terminology of the CWS can be understood as *depersonalising*, in that it fails to capture important aspects of people's lives. The concepts reduce complexity. Using them results in simplification and categorisation of life situations and conditions for growing up, and this can be both necessary and practical in the work of the CWS.

However, the concepts are also valid outside the child welfare system. Since they are not neutral, they steer the understanding of a given phenomenon in a certain direction. "Foster child", for example, like "stepchild" and "adopted child", marks a division between the status of these children as compared with biological children in a family. The term "foster child" further creates associations with being disadvantaged and in danger of distorted development, despite the fact that many children in foster care are just like most other children and have no special difficulties.[7] The use of these terms can therefore contribute to the upholding of crude concepts of problem and deviance, to the marginalisation of children and young people and to the division between "normal children" and "foster children".

Given the challenges posed by the system language used by the CWS we have sought to use a more neutral language in this book. Rather than using the term "foster child" we mostly write "children growing up in foster care". This is also more in line with usage among the children who participated in our studies, where hardly anybody referred to themselves as foster children. We have, however, chosen to stay with concepts like "foster parents". This is largely because of the limitations of language; we have no other descriptive terms for the role of, for example, grandparents who assume the care of grandchildren, or for the situation of children who grow up with their aunt in the custody of the CWS.

Kinship care – family and kin

Another concept we need to clarify is kinship care. The term indicates that the phenomenon refers to both family and kin. For some, these two words will trigger different associations, while for others they will mean the same. This is what happened when an uncle and aunt in our study were asked to make a list of who they considered to be the family of their 12-year-old nephew whom they were fostering. Once completed, their lists were compared. The uncle began by explaining:

UNCLE: Well, it's just the nuclear family, isn't it, and grandparents. That's family …
AUNT: Haven't you included us?
UNCLE: No, I just –

AUNT: Don't you consider *us* to be his family?
UNCLE: Well, sort of … Because we're obviously related…
AUNT: Yes, but since we've practically been, that is, assumed the role of his parents, surely –
UNCLE: Yes, but … (…) That means you're including all the relatives.
AUNT: Yes, people who care …
UNCLE: OK … But I have a much narrower view of what family means.
AUNT: Yes, obviously (laughs a little). Doesn't even include us! Oh, well, that's –
UNCLE: But really, it's a difference of principle, but, well …I just call it family, but it kind of means kin, that's it.

The conversation between the uncle and aunt illustrates that relatives and family are not always understood as unambiguous terms for clearly defined phenomena. For that reason, we need to clarify the meaning given to the terms in this book. Let us start with the notion of kinship. By kinship we mean relationships which in a broad sense can be traced back to biological or legal bonds, such as marriage or adoption. The term *kinship care* thus means foster care where the child has biological or legal bonds to one or both foster parents. In our culture, kinship is often understood as an "objective" phenomenon, in the sense that such relationships can be defined based on "external" characteristics not depending on whether the social relationship is understood as close or distant. You would regard a cousin or an aunt as your kin, even if you had never met, or hardly ever see, the person. So, we see that the notion of kinship can evoke associations to distant family relations. The notion of family, on the other hand, evokes associations to what is everyday and close. That is one of the reasons the notion of family is so important in this book.

Just like the notion of kinship, family is commonly defined in terms of biological and legal bonds, but generally, 'household' is also an important criterion. The following definition is from Statistics Norway:

> A family consists of individuals living in the same house and connected to each other as marriage partners, registered partners, co-habitants, and/or as parents and children (regardless of the age of the child).

> (SSB, 2019)

The foster care agreement is a formal juridical contract which incorporates the child into *the* family. In everyday speech, the notion of family is thus close to the characteristics of the nuclear family, in that members of *the* family are defined using fixed criteria. In the absence of a more precise concept, we do use the term 'family' like this in the book, for example, when discussing several different families who are all part of the child's kin. Most importantly – from a theoretical and analytical standpoint – we use 'family' in line with more recent sociological theory. In this book that means recognising that kinship care consists of a range of different family types and relationships which are created through action and which change over time. Such an open and plurivalent definition exceeds the criteria in the definition from Statistics Norway, and is essential in order to understand the variation, change and complexity found in kinship care.

This excerpt from a letter we received from a maternal grandmother who took part in our study illustrates the relationship between the notions of kinship and family:

> After a difficult year (...) things changed dramatically. I took her with me to my mother in Northern Norway, which is also where my three siblings and most of the nieces and nephews are with their families. We spent four weeks there, and Jenny, who in her first seven years had had a family of five: [her] mum, her brother, me and uncle John and his live-in partner, discovered that she had several aunts and uncles and more than twenty second cousins, and they were *all* her *family*. After that summer, there was a change in her personality. Now, after a summer in Northern Norway with a lot of family around her, she has caught up with her age in every way. She is a completely normal 8-year-old, who knows almost everything in this world.

What the maternal grandmother is describing here is how kinship is re-defined by lived, everyday experiences. The excerpt illustrates how kinship carries cultural norms and values which can lead to social relationships being perceived as close. In this example, the interpretation of the relationships changed from kinship to family.

How the book is structured

The book is divided into seven chapters, including this introduction. Chapter 2 places growing up with relatives in an historical child protection context. The aim of the chapter is to illuminate some of the most central developments in the 100-year-old history of the Norwegian CWS up to the institutionalisation of kinship care as an intervention and category in child protection. We show how child welfare has gone through several periods of varying policies and ideologies. The chapter ends with a discussion of the factors that led to the current prioritisation of kinship care as an intervention in child welfare.

In Chapter 3 the focus is on research. As previously mentioned, kinship care as a research topic did not emerge until the 1990s in the USA. At a time of strong growth in the number of kinship placements, but very limited knowledge of kinship care, there was a demand for knowledge about the impact of kinship, compared with non-kinship care. This resulted in a concentration of evaluative research on kinship care, generally as compared with non-kinship care. Based on systematic reviews we show the results of this research and discuss its limitations. We call for further research which uses different methodological approaches and raises different issues for discussion. We put forward the argument that there is a particular need for further research on foster care as family, which investigates its variation and complexity and which includes the perspectives of the children, the parents and the foster parents.

Unlike the norm in non-kinship care, kinship care, in the main, is based on established relationships between the relatives who have entered into a kinship care contract, that is to say the foster parents and the child and the child's mother or father. The similarity with non-kinship care is that kinship care is governed by the same regulations. In Chapter 4 we use various theoretical perspectives to look at the contrasting logic that kinship care families have to relate to, and show how kinship care may be experienced, both as an intervention and as a family.

In Chapter 5 we look into who become kinship foster parents and what the reasons for accepting this responsibility might be. We show that kinship care can be understood as both a predominantly female and a working-class phenomena, in the sense that it is mainly the child's maternal female relatives, with lower educational and income levels compared to non-kinhsip foster parents, who become kinship foster parents. Responsibility, duty and solidarity are some of the key reasons for assuming such a responsibility. A close relationship with the child may be another significant factor, and one which leads to mostly close relatives becoming kinship foster parents.

Investigating kinship care as family requires theoretical perspectives linked to family life. These are provided in Chapter 6 through family sociological perspectives. In the first half of the chapter we outline the changing understanding of family and relationships, from the 1950s until today. The second part describes the experiences of teenagers and young adults growing up in kinship care. Like other studies where

children, teenagers and young adults were interviewed, the informants in our study emphasised normality as a characteristic when they
talked about upbringing and family life. In this chapter we discuss
how normality is understood in this context, and why it is an asset.

In the last chapter of the book, Chapter 7, we gather up all the loose
ends and direct the attention to possible opportunities for development and change in kinship care and point to the need for further research into this phenomenon.

All the chapters in the book are jointly written by Jeanette
Skoglund, Renee Thørnblad and Amy Holtan.

Notes

1 Statistics Norway has a wide definition of the category foster care. In
 addition to municipal foster homes, it includes state foster homes and
 emergency shelters. These two are alternatives to institutions, and are not
 foster homes which receive children who need foster homes to grow up
 in. When we calculate the extent of kinship care, we are including only
 the following two types of intervention: foster care in families and close
 networks, and foster care outside families and close networks. At the end
 of 2020, 9,980 children and young people aged 0–22 were living in foster
 care in and outside family and close networks, whereof 3,239 in family and
 6,741 outside family and close networks. If we include emergency shelters,
 state foster homes, etc., there were in total 11,098 children and young people aged 0–22 living in the category defined by Statistics Norway as foster
 care at the end of 2020.
2 The project is funded by the Regional Centre for Child and Youth Mental
 Health and Child Welfare – North, Faculty of Health Sciences, UiT the
 Arctic University of Norway, Tromsø.
3 Prior to the data collection points in the project, each single study received
 the required approval from the Regional Committee for Medical and
 Health Research Ethics (REK) and the Norwegian Centre for Research
 Data (NSD).
4 The other study was carried out in Denmark (Egelund, Jakobsen, & Steen,
 2010; Knudsen, 2009).
5 *CBCL*: Child behavioural checklist, *PSI*: Parenting stress index and *ASR*:
 Adult self-report.
6 According to the Child Welfare Act, Section 4–7, parents can leave the
 child in the care of others in a private placement. The Norwegian CWS
 can, on certain conditions, demand that the home must be approved as
 a foster home. There is no overview of the number of private placements
 in accordance with Section 4–7. Unlike in countries such as the USA, the
 UK and Spain, informal kinship care has not been given much attention
 in Norway and the other Nordic countries.
7 As an example, a Norwegian study of 270 children aged 6–12 who were
 living in foster care showed that 49 percent of the children did not have
 any mental/psychiatric problems (Lehmann, Havik, Havik, & Heiervang,
 2013).

12 Introduction

References

Andenæs, A. (2011). From 'placement' to 'a child on the move': Methodological strategies to give children a more central position in Child Welfare Service. *Qualitative Social Work, 11*(5), 486–501. doi:10.1177/1473325011408174.

Egelund, T., Jakobsen, T. B., & Steen, L. (2010). *"Det er jo min familie!" Beretninger fra børn og unge i slægtspleje.* (Rapport nr. 10:34). København: SFI.

Holtan, A. (2002). *Barndom i fosterhjem i egen slekt.* (Doctoral dissertation). University of Tromsø, Norway.

Knudsen, L. (2009). *Børn og unge anbragt i slægten. En sammenligning af slægtsanbringelser og anbringelser i traditionel familiepleje.* (Rapport nr. 09:26). København: SFI.

Lehmann, S., Havik, O. E., Havik, T., & Heiervang, E. R. (2013). Mental disorders in foster children: A study of prevalence, comorbidity and risk factors. *Child and Adolescent Psychiatry and Mental Health, 7*(39). doi: 10.1186/1753-2000-7-39.

Moldestad, B. (1996). *Egne barn – andres unger? En undersøkelse om sosialarbeideres mening om fosterbarns familie som plasseringssted.* (Hovedoppgave i sosialt arbeid). Norges teknisk-naturvitenskapelige universitet (NTNU).

Norges forskningsråd (1997). *Perspektivnotat: delprogram Barnevernforskning 1997–2001* (O. f. k. o. s. Norges forskningsråd Ed.). Oslo: Norges forskningsråd, Området for kultur og samfunn.

Skoglund, J. (2018). *Upbringing by relatives: Incorporating new understandings and perspectives into the study of kinship foster care.* (Doktoravhandling). Universitetet i Tromsø – Norges arktiske universitet.

Statistics Norway/Statistisk sentralbyrå (SSB) (2019). *Familier og husholdninger.* (Om statistikken. Viktige begrep og variabler). Retrieved from https://www.ssb.no/familie.

Statistics Norway/Statistisk sentralbyrå (SSB) (2021). *Barnevern, 2020.* (Tabell 5: Barnevernstiltak per 31. desember etter tiltak). Retrieved from https://www.ssb.no/barneverng/.

Sundt, H. (2012). *Slektsfosterhjem i Norden – opplæring og oppfølging.* Retrieved from Oslo.

Thørnblad, R. (2011). *Slektsfosterhjem – offentlig tiltak i private hjem.* (Doktoravhandling). Universitetet i Tromsø.

Vinnerljung, B. (1996). *Fosterbarn som vuxna.* Lund, Sverige: Arkiv Förlag.

Winokur, M., Holtan, A., & Batchelder, K. E. (2014). Kinship care for the safety, permanency, and well-being of children removed from the home for maltreatment. *Cochrane Database of Systematic Reviews, Issue 1. Art. No.: CD006546.* doi:10.1002/14651858.CD006546.pub3.

Winokur, M., Holtan, A., & Valentine, D. (2009). Kinship care for the safety, permanency, and well-being of children removed from the home for maltreatment. *Cochrane Database of Systematic Reviews, Issue 1. Art. No.: CD006546.* Retrieved from http://db.c2admin.org/doc-pdf/Winokur_Kinshipcare_review.pdf. doi:10.1002/14651858.CD006546.pub2.

2 Kinship care in an historical child protection context

From poor relief to child welfare services

Foster care as an official child welfare intervention goes back over a century in Norway. The history of private and partly official arrangements for children who, for various reasons, were unable to live with their birth parents does not commence with the establishment of the CWS. As far back as the 12th century, poor relief was introduced as a form of official child protection. The main principle was that families were responsible for their own; however, farm owners were obliged to provide food and shelter for children and elders, or pay a fee in order to be exempt, in cases where families did not take care of their own (Hagen, 2004, p. 10). From 1900 until the present day, Norwegian society has undergone significant changes which have also made its mark on the CWS. The services have been through several distinct periods – from poor relief and later protection of the defenceless in the early 1900s, via professionalisation from the 1960s, to the current knowledge-based, partly market-oriented child welfare system.

From the 1980s there has been a strong differentiation of the welfare services offered. The Norwegian CWS were separated from the health and social services and established as a separate agency and have since been subject to extensive reforms. Governance models inspired by New Public Management, based on principles using the market as a model, have been introduced. Goals and outcomes are evaluated based on observable criteria, such as deadline compliance, whether fixed numbers of follow-up visits and supervisions have been carried out, and the existence of care planning.

Another feature of this development is the privatisation of CWS. Private actors, both non-profit and commercial, are now operating in foster care, recruitment and follow-up. According to Vista Analyse, in 2014–2015, 77 percent of the country's CWS used private actors to

DOI: 10.4324/9781003231363-2

carry out one or more of the services that local authorities are legally required to provide (Ekhaugen & Rasmussen, 2016, p. 7).

Individualisation has made its mark on children's services in most Western countries. This has resulted in increased attention on the individual child rather than on families, networks and local communities. In the field of foster care, it means that the main focus of the work of the CWS is on helping the child as an individual to adjust to a new family. Kinship care could be said to represent an alternative to individualisation, in that biology, social relationships and kinship are given greater emphasis.

The term "child welfare as a mirror of society" (Ericsson, 1996) and its implied perspectives are relevant for child welfare studies and for the development of non-kinship and kinship care. The term refers to the changes in child welfare prioritisation reflecting changes in society as a whole. Using the notion of "child welfare as societal protection", Stang Dahl (1978) claimed that as a public body, the CWS uphold and defend the dominant attitudes and values which at any time are in evidence, and consequently contribute to upholding society's status quo. As we see it, both of these perspectives are relevant for the understanding of child welfare interventions in general and non-kinship and kinship care in particular.

The first Child Welfare Act

The idea of "placement" reflects the power of the authorities to move a child. From the early 1900s, what was then referred to as "putting children away" increasingly became a matter for the State. The 1896 Child Welfare Act (implemented in 1900) made Norway the first country with specific legislation for the protection and welfare of children. Prior to this there were various types of poor relief, such as parish relief, workhouses, orphanages and almshouses, regulated by various sections of the law (Hagen, 2001; Midré, 1990).[1] The aim of the 1896 Act was first and foremost to protect society from mischievous and morally neglected children (Ericsson, 2002). The children were to be taken care of for the required upbringing and education. A child custody committee had the power to remove the child from its home, deprive the parents of control of the child and put the child away. The Child Welfare Act of 1896 cemented the care of neglected children as a matter for the authorities (Seip, 1994a, p. 112).

The 1896 Act covered children who, according to Seip (1994a, p. 212), "had committed crimes or immoral actions, those who were recalcitrant truants, those neglected by those who should care for them and those who could be expected to become morally depraved" – so guilty, innocent and potentially guilty children. Most of the applications to the child custody committees came from the police and from schools, and only rarely from authorities or the parents (Hagen, 2001, p. 63). The custody committees thus had a socio-political and a penological function, and putting children away in accordance with the 1896 Act should not primarily involve poor relief (Mykland & Masdalen, 1987, p. 150).

According to Hagen (2001), the 1896 Act was intended as a step in the direction of separating child welfare from the poor-law authorities. The aim was that the child custody committees should take over the responsibility when it came to the placement of children. That, however, did not happen. Instead, a two-part system which lasted over 50 years was put in place. According to Hagen (2001), the children were arbitrarily placed, and the interventions under the auspices of the child custody committees and the poor-law authorities were in the main just the same.

Increased official engagement in the "putting away" of children resulted in the significant change that the authorities were obliged to control the practice by exercising supervision. The first follow-up studies of children from the child custody committees were published in the 1930s. Diagnostic tests showed a partly deprived and heterogenous group in terms of intellectual ability and physical condition. Results from the industrial schools (*skolehjem*) compared with family care showed that those who had been in foster homes had a more favourable (i.e. more law-abiding) development (Thuen, 2002, p. 357). From then on, all foster care was to be supervised. The background to this was increased scrutiny of the conditions of the children in foster care, including legal action against foster parents who had neglected the children in their care. There were many reasons why people requested to become foster parents: from the wish to have a child of their own to financial motives and the need for cheap labour. Hagen (2001) refers to the following newspaper advertisement from 1925:

> Vang child custody committee have a number of boys aged 8–15 for hire. Please contact the Administrator for the Poor to make an offer.

The chairman of Oslo Child Custody Committee deemed the advertisement both illegal and improper and reported it to the Ministry.[2]

A number of different sciences and professions have contributed to the establishment and development of the Norwegian CWS.

The original child welfare legislation came about as a result of collaboration between criminology, law and education around 1900. Tove Stang Dahl (1978, p. 10) described the CWS as a concept and interventions as its execution to protect society, created in the late 19th century when the state was expected to intervene in social problems. Urban poverty recruited a growing number of "depraved and neglected" children to both prisons and schools. The educators wanted the children out of the schools and the criminologists wanted the children out of the prisons (Stang Dahl, 1978). The medical profession with its emphasis on hygiene and health was also greatly influential in the early years of the CWS. From the 1920s and 1930s pedagogy and psychology also gained influence (Blom, 2004; Seip, 1994b).

Foster care and institutions – gender-based practice

History tells us that a child's gender has been important in the choice of placement. Between 1900 and 1950, boys, especially the oldest, were more frequently placed in foster care than girls. This was often foster care on farms, which availed themselves of the labour provided by the boys. The youngest girls were more sought after in homes where the desire for a child outweighed the need for labour or profit (Andresen, 2006, pp. 56–60).

The child welfare institutions were usually gender-based, and the education and upbringing had a clear class and gender bias. During the first half of the 20th century, the educational aim was for the boys and girls to adjust to their place in society, that is to say as workers, servants and housewives (Andresen, 2006). Boys who were placed in institutions often faced a stricter regime than girls in line with the belief at the time that boys needed a "firmer hand" (Hagen, 2001; Jon, 2007). The practice of gender-based sanction systems in the institutions was linked to the control of the criminal actions of boys and the sexuality of girls (Ericsson, 2002).

The 1953 Child Welfare Act; the "disciplinarian" is replaced by science

The protection of children versus the protection of the interests of society, whether to treat or to punish, use force or rely on voluntariness, have all, throughout history, been topics in the debates about the foundation of child welfare legislation. In the debate about the child custody system, there was frequent criticism of the CWS' covert penal tasks within educational and treatment institutions (Ericsson,

1996; Stang Dahl, 1978). The term "child protection" emerged in the inter-war period and was incorporated into the 1953 Child Welfare Act (Hagen, 2004, p. 9). One significant objective of the 1953 Act was to re-purpose the disciplinarian's moralising custody committee as a service for helping and protecting children. In the legislation, the moralistic formulations of the 1896 Act were replaced with scientific concepts. The aim of the new Child Welfare Act – universal responsibility for the living conditions of all children and support for families – marked a departure from the 1896 Act. Damning descriptions of parents and children and their problems were replaced by scientific language, in particular from medicine and psychiatry. The intention was to assist, not to coerce (Larsen, 2002, p. 103). The "care" concept replaced "upbringing", and the term "care order", which is still used today, was introduced. The Child Welfare Boards replaced the custody committees.

The 1953 Act placed great emphasis on family protection by taking "the best interests of the child" and "the biological principle" as the starting point of any child protection intervention. The best interests of the child implied that consideration for the child had to be the decisive factor in the choice of intervention; in other words, the needs of the child had to be safeguarded. Ideas of the best interests of the child must also be understood in the light of developmental psychology which gained ground from the 1950s, and which placed great emphasis on the bonds between parents (especially the mother) and children. The biological principle was based on the fundamental value that the best interest of the child was to grow up with their biological parents. Parents had the primary responsibility for the child and the right and duty to ensure that the child was given the required care (Haugli, 2000). The placement of children outside the home was to be a last resort after other measures in the home had been tried (Official Report NOU 2000: 12). The biological principle is still given great importance in children's services, as we will come back to later in this chapter.

The Act provided regulations for preventive measures in the home with the aim of keeping the family together. Poverty was no longer a legitimate reason for a child to be taken into care. Preventive measures such as financial support or supervision were intended to enable, as far as possible, children to grow up with their parents (Larsen, 2002). The number and extent of preventive measures grew strongly, and in the mid-1970s preventive measures overtook as a first intervention in child protection cases (Ericsson, 2002, p. 37). The main emphasis in the work of the child protection services has since then been interventions for children who are living with their parents. At the end of

2018, a total of 39,043 children and young people were registered as receiving interventions form children's services. Among children and young people who received child protection interventions, 23,903 (61 percent) were living with their parents, and 15,140 (39 percent) were placed outside the home (8,868 as custody interventions and 6,272 as support interventions) (SSB, 2021b).

The 1992 Child Welfare Act: individualisation and the child's perspective

Two important changes came with the 1992 Act: the child was given the status of a separate legal personality, and any initiative from the CWS was to be based on the minimal intervention principle. The latter implies that more comprehensive intervention is not to be used until a less intrusive approach has been tried. Intervention in the child's home must be tried or considered before a care order can be placed on the child. The intention of avoiding care orders and placement of the child continued. What the 1953 Act referred to as "preventive measures" now came to be known as "support measures", and they could be put in place earlier than the 1953 Act allowed. The 1992 Act also paved the way for foster homes to be used as a support measure, that is to say that the birth parents, and not necessarily the CWS, had formal custody of the child. The legal basis of foster homes can thus be both as a support measure and as a custody intervention.

The United Nations Convention on the Rights of the Child, which is from this period, reinforced the rights of the child and their position as a legal subject. The Convention was ratified by the UN General Assembly in 1980, and by Norway in 1991, and incorporated into Norwegian law in 2003. Article 3.1 of the Convention states that the best interests of the child must be a primary consideration for all actions concerning children (Ministry of Children and Family Affairs, 2003, p. 9). The incorporation into Norwegian law gave children a stronger legal position, including in child protection cases. Children's right to participation is laid down in law. The basic principle is that a child over the age of 15 has the rights of a party to their case. As far as foster care is concerned, "children over the age of 7 and younger children who are able to form their own opinion shall be informed and given the opportunity to be heard" before foster care is chosen. "The child's opinion shall be taken into account in accordance with the age and maturity of the child". The former understanding of the child as an object to be helped, developed into the child as a subject with its own rights.

The work on law reform between 1900 and the 1992 Child Welfare Act reflects prevailing ideologies and the development of a society characterised by increased individualisation, and the emphasis is still very much on the child as an individual today.

Reforms and work on new child welfare legislation

On 1 July 2018 it was established by law that the CWS must always consider whether anyone in the child's family or close network could be chosen as foster carers (Section 4–22 of the Child Welfare Act). It was further established by law that the CWS shall enable the use of tools and methods for network involvement in foster care work should this be appropriate. In Official Report NOU 2018: 18 it was also proposed that local authorities should be obliged always to consider whether the child can move into a foster home in, or close to, their own municipality. These strategies are intended to reinforce the child's proximity both to their own networks and to the CWS who are responsible for the care of the child (Table 2.1).

Changing priorities of institutions and foster care from 1900 until today

The types of placement which ought to be given priority have been a subject for discussion since the 1900s. The debate about placing children in foster care versus institutions had begun in Norway and other parts of Europe long before the 1892 Act (Thuen, 2002). Eilert Sundt[3] argued as early as 1870 that a foster home was the most appropriate place to grow up:

> The best way to bring up children is in the midst of a family and in family life; and if this is true for children in general, it is particularly true for mischievous children. I am certain that I am right in saying that it is especially the naughty children who require the most diligent and best upbringing methods, that is in the family and in normal life, and this cannot be replaced by a monastery-like institution or by any kind of asylum created by humans, however well-meaning this might be.

Sundt stressed the importance of careful choice, not random selection, of foster families. Another important actor in the debate about institution versus foster care in the second half of the 19th century was the philanthropist Christen C. Møller, who, unlike Sundt, argued in

Table 2.1 Child welfare legislation over a period, a few characteristics

1896 Child Welfare Act (*Vergerådsloven*)	• Children under the age of 16 (from the 1930s, 18) can be "placed away [from home]" for upbringing and education. • Primary focus: protecting society • Children's homes, asylums
1953 Child Welfare Act	• Professional and science-based influences • From upbringing to care. Introduction of the concept of care orders. • The best interests of the child • The biological principle. Children should primarily grow up with their parents. • Preventive measures and family protection • Foster care and adoption
1992 Child Welfare Act	• The child's status as a separate legal personality • The principle of the most minimal intervention • Support measures replace preventive measures • Foster care as a support measure • Intervention models
2021 Child Welfare Act	• Strengthening of children's participation • Extension of after care (from 23 to 25) • The obligation of local authorities to seek foster care among kin and networks laid down in law. • Importance of sibling relationships • Methodical work and standardisation of procedures

favour of the "rescue asylum" and claimed that foster care was unnatural: "With one's own kin one seeks the heart, with others one seeks a living" (sitert i Thuen, 2002, p. 223). Based on this thinking, a child in foster care would commonly be a source of income, not a source of love or belonging. The child would therefore take second place in the foster family, thereby giving the foster parents only limited influence. We see from this that the complicating factor of fundamentally different views on caring for children in and outside their family was apparent even at that early stage. The emotional bonds of a biological family were considered irreplaceable, and at the same time the family served as an ideal model and a yardstick for establishments that were safeguarding other people's children. The relationship between caring for children and economic interests is another topic which has been debated throughout the ages, and which is also topical today (see

Chapter 4 for a theoretical and empirical elaboration of the relationship between foster care and money).

Despite earlier revelations of neglect and abuse, child welfare institutions as arenas for children to grow up in experienced something of a "golden age" in the inter-war years (Andresen, 2006, p. 26). This was also the period of professionalisation of children's services and commitment to institutions such as children's homes, industrial schools and workhouses (Seip, 1994b, p. 74). Children's homes were regarded as the optimal placement alternative because they offered the opportunity for better state control of the enterprise than foster care and provided the children with better education, schooling and a more secure childhood. The growth of youth crime, however, led to an increase in the number of care orders during this period, and the supply of children's home placements was overtaken by the demand (Hagen, 2001, p. 111). When it also emerged that the costs of running an institution far exceeded that of foster care, the expansion was scaled down in many municipalities (Andresen, 2006). Revelations that children's homes were run more like "total institutions"[4] than as homes for the children, and that children were sometimes exposed to neglect and abuse even in state-controlled children's homes, also contributed to a renewed focus on foster care placements. The number of institutions had thus been considerably reduced by 1946 (Ericsson, 2002; Simonsen & Ericsson, 2005). The 1947 Child Protection Committee commissioned an overview of the placement sites of all children in care in Norway (see Table 2.2).

In other words, the rise and fall of the child welfare institution took place over a relatively short period. Since then, placements in institutions have gradually declined. From the 1953 Child Welfare Act, and continuing today, a reduction in the use of institution placements is an expressed socio-political goal. This shift away from institutions and towards foster care has been significant in the professionalisation of the foster care system in terms of paid work and competency development.

Table 2.2 Placement sites for children in care in Norway in 1947 (Hagen, 2001, p. 74)

	Boys	*Girls*	*Total*
Foster care	1,616 (56.6%)	1,480 (60%)	3,096 (58.2%)
Children's homes	1,239 (43.4%)	986 (40%)	2,225 (41.8%)
	2,855 (100%)	2,466 (100%)	5,321 (100%)

Adoption as an alternative to foster care

Since as far back as the 1896 Act, foster care has been an intervention between institutionalisation and adoption. Until the Second World War, adoption was not frequently used for "putting children away". Andresen (2006, p. 194) claimed that the main reason for this was consideration for the "mother and morals" rather than consideration for the child. This implied that unmarried mothers should not be let off taking responsibility for their child, even if the child was "put away". Adoption became far more common during and after the War and reached a peak in the 1960s (Andresen, 2006; Ingvaldsen, 2001). "The best interests of the child" and new psychological theories on the mother-child relationship which were part of the professional knowledge at the time lent professional support to adoption. Out of consideration not only for the child, but also for other parties, it was considered best that children who were not to grow up with their mother were moved as early as possible (Simonsen & Ericsson, 2005). The post-war family ideology of the nuclear family and the ideal housewife may also have increased the demand for children by childless couples (Andresen, 2006).

The decline in adoption in the 1960s and 1970s came about partly as a result of welfare reforms (such as single parent benefit, better access to contraceptives and abortion and nursery schools), and partly because of changes in norms and perceptions, which meant that unmarried mothers and their children were not stigmatised to the same degree as before. The expanded commitment of the CWS to preventing official care orders may also have contributed to the reduction in the number of adoptions. Nowadays, adoptions of children born in Norway are extremely rare. During the period 2011–2016, an average of 0.6 percent of children in foster care were adopted (Helland & Skivenes, 2019, p. 39). According to Statistics Norway, there were a total of 36 adoptions of children and young people in foster care in 2020 (SSB, 2021a).

Increased emphasis on foster care

In the first half of the 20th century, the child-rearing goals of institutions were linked to the interests of society rather than the needs of the individual child (Stang Dahl, 1978). Assistance for disadvantaged groups had clear elements of surveillance and discipline (Weihe, 2004). The children were to be taught how to become useful members of society, that is to say industrious, demure and clean workers. Later, the fundamental shift in the view of children and child labour which led to the belief that children should not work, but go to school, play and have time to themselves, had consequences for the use of foster care. Child development was considered important, and this was something which the family was thought to be better suited to safeguarding than child welfare institutions. The post-war economic growth meant that foster families no longer had the same need as before for the cheap labour sometimes provided by children in care. At the same time, family policy in the post-war period influenced the prioritisation of foster care over child welfare institutions. Gradually the attention was beginning to focus on the needs of the individual child. The idea was for the resources of the foster family to meet the needs of the child.

With the 1953 Child Welfare Act, the ideal was that children who could not live with their birth parents got a new family. The foster family was to be a nuclear family, with a foster mother and a foster father, known as a functional family, as a replacement for the dysfunctional family. The nuclear family ideal played an important part in the thinking about family for children – thinking which is still important today. Section 24 of the 1953 Act stated: "For children who are considered suitable a place should primarily be sought in a good foster home". Social policy gradually changed from the idea of children growing up in children's homes. Stays in an institution should now, unlike previously, be as short as possible, and the design and operation of children's homes should as far as possible be modelled on the family and family homes (Ericsson, 2002). In order to counteract the stigmatisation of children in the care of social services, interventions should be integrated or designed in such a way that they appeared as everyday and normal as possible – whether in or outside the family.

In the wake of the increased importance of foster care, the 1953 Act recommended the establishment of inter-municipal foster care centres in order to facilitate and coordinate the work on the "placement" of children. Organisations were able to provide assistance with this work; however, private enterprises were prohibited from actually running operations concerned with the placement of children outside the home (Mykland & Masdalen, 1987, p. 151). The privatisation and commercialisation of tasks such as recruitment, remuneration and follow-up of foster homes that we are used to today are thus a recent phenomenon.

Sköld (2011) analysed the norms for good foster care in Sweden through handbooks written for practitioners in the period 1903–2003. In these books, the authors described the criteria for the choice of foster homes. Sköld's point was that the characteristics sought in foster parents, as well as those to avoid, constituted demarcations for the understanding of normal parenthood in the period in question. From

1900 until 1929, the minimum criterion for the choice of foster home was the avoidance of "bad" families. There were no requirements for the child to be an equal family member, nor any mention that being a foster mother was acceptable as a job. From 1930 until around 1960, the nuclear family was dominated by ideals of motherhood which implied a close mother-child relationship. In the field of foster care, the emphasis was gradually placed on the matching of foster mother and child in order for them to be able to develop a close mother-child relationship. In terms of age, the foster mother should have been able to be the child's mother, and her class background was to be like that of the child. In accordance with the nuclear family ideal, the foster mother had to be a housewife, particularly for pre-school children. The child was the responsibility of the foster mother. In the period from 1960 until around 1980, the nuclear family ideal was still strong, but fathers were now given greater importance as caregivers and educators, both when it came to the choice of foster home and follow-up after placement. From around 1980 it was considered important that foster parents had a secure financial position, a stable relationship with each other, physical capability and a social network. Children with immigrant backgrounds should not be placed in their own culture if that contravened the prevailing norms of parenthood.

Is it safe to assume that this Swedish study can be transferred to the Norwegian context? Throughout large parts of the 20th century Norway was a poorer country than Sweden; however, the development of the welfare state had similar features and there is reason to believe that the Swedish norms of parenthood were not significantly different from those in Norway. Sköld's study demonstrated how the value placed on the position of the child was expressed in the CWS. From around the Second World War there was gradually a greater emphasis on children's emotional care. The study also illustrated the conservative, gender-based practice of the children's services, where women were regarded as the central caregiver, and where the nuclear family was considered the desired family type. Statements given in hearings in connection with changes to the regulations of foster care in Norway confirmed the dominant status of the nuclear family in foster care work. Analysis of our data from T1 also showed that traditional gender-based practices were widespread (Holtan & Thørnblad, 2009).

Foster care at the heart of child welfare services

In 2016 the Norwegian parliament approved the first White Paper on foster care (Norwegian Ministry of Children, Equality and Social

Inclusion, 2016). The report expressed the important position of foster care in current CWS. It also paved the way for foster care to be further developed as a child welfare intervention through systems for the recruitment, reporting, follow-up of children, birth parents and foster parents, and framework conditions for foster care. Foster care was to be further professionalised through both competency development and work regulations for foster parents in some types of foster care. Advice from children and young people was included in the report's introduction. The statements below are from user organisations of children with experience of CWS:

- We ask you to find foster parents who are fond of children and who can show us love.
- We ask you to find foster parents who will understand the importance of contact with siblings and family.
- Let us feel that we are wanted, loved and taken care of.

To continue the work of the Report to the Storting (White Paper) on foster care, a committee was set up to consider the framework conditions for foster care. In Official Report NOU 2018: 18 A secure framework for foster care (2018, p. 13), the committee establishes an understanding of foster care first and foremost as family, just like other families. They claim, on the one hand, that there is not necessarily a discrepancy between professionalisation of the caregiving role in the sense of training and support for the foster family and the role of parents, although this involves a balancing act. On the other hand the committee claims that foster families are different from other families in certain specific areas, in that they have taken on a responsibility from the CWS. The committee's emphasis on family aspects reflects the fact that contributions from the user organisations for children and young people have won approval in certain areas which may have an impact on policy making in the field of foster care.

Contact between parents and their children in care, visitation rights

Until the end of the Second World War, parents and relatives had an uncertain and unpredictable place in the lives of the children who had been taken into care. Contact with the children's families was regulated by the child welfare institutions and varied greatly. In some cases siblings might be placed together, but there were only limited opportunities to do this. Some children's homes limited contact between children and their families as far as possible, while others facilitated a certain level of contact and mutual visitation. The restrictions were often based on assessments of whether contact with family and relatives would have a negative impact on the children. Another reason for limited contact might have been a desire to curtail the access of third parties to life in the institutions. In foster homes, the children's birth parents may have been perceived as interfering or as competition for the foster parents, and therefore kept at a distance. In such cases parents may have preferred for the child to be placed in a children's home, since that would make it easier to maintain contact (Andresen, 2006; Pettersen, 2005).

As previously mentioned, since the 1950s, psychology, and in particular developmental psychology, has been instrumental in the practice, legislation and knowledge development of the CWS. In psychology, there have been opposing schools of thought in the understanding of the child's relationship with their biological parents. Since the 1970s, two theories in particular have been important: the attachment theory and the object relations theory. Attachment theory, in particular represented by Goldstein, Freud and Solnit (1973), broadly claims that biological parents can be exchanged and that the child is able to become attached to new psychological parents. Their book, *Beyond the Best Interests of the Child*, provoked a great debate on parental welfare versus child welfare. According to this theory, children placed in long-term foster care ought to be given space and time to form an attachment to their new psychological parents. Contact with their biological parents is therefore not regarded as essential. The other theory, represented by, for example, Bengt Börjeson and his colleagues in the project "Children in Crisis", emphasises the significance of the child's early interaction with biological parents (Börjeson, Magnberg, Nording, & Persson, 1976; Cederström & Hessle, 1980). According to this view the child's parents cannot be replaced; they are and will always be the psychological parents, including after a separation. Children's services must therefore actively work for the child to be able to live at home. When it does become necessary for the child to be put into care, contact must be maintained between children and parents through regular visits. According to this perspective it is necessary for the foster parents to acknowledge the child's relationship with their parents.

From the 2000s, attachment theory based on development psychology has been established as essential to the theoretical platform of the CWS. This was strongly emphasised in Official Report NOU 2012: 5 *Better protection of children's development*. In this report the committee proposed replacing the "biological principle" with a new principle defined as "development-supportive attachment". This implies that when assessing care orders and re-placements, the CWS must consider whether the attachment and relationship quality between the caregivers and children supports the child's development or not. Attachment theory talks about secure and insecure attachment. The child can also be attached to those who hurt them, thereby having an insecure attachment. Having been placed in care, the child can develop attachment to new caregivers. This perspective is mainly based on the studies of Mary Ainsworth (1973). Attachment theory is widely used in the CWS. The term "attachment" is used in legislation and exists side by side, with the emphasis on family and networks. One criticism of attachment theory and the child services' use of it is the lack of support in the form of empirical research for this perspective.

Visitation rights were established by law for the first time in Norway in the children's acts of 1956. Prior to that an administrative practice had been developed whereby parents were given visiting access in cases of divorce. In 1969 this became primarily a right for the child. The 1981 Children Act opened the door for this to be extended to all children regardless of the parents' status when the child was born. Since around 1989, all children and parents have mutual visitation rights. In child protection legislation, visitation rights are first dealt with in the 1992 Act (Haugli, 2000, pp. 74–76). Today, the child's contact with parents following a care order is safeguarded, for example, by the obligation of the CWS to facilitate contact. The need for foster parents to collaborate with the CWS and birth parents in order to reach contact agreements is therefore emphasised. The official report NOU 2016: 16 proposes extending the right of contact to the child's siblings and others close to the child. "The child welfare services shall, where this is not contradicted by consideration for the child, facilitate contact with siblings" (Section 4–16). Attachment theory is also strongly present in the decision-making of contact arrangements.

We see from this that society's changing ideas of parenthood and of the best interests of the child are reflected in the practical work of the CWS. Generalised concepts of visiting and contact between parents and children are today institutionalised by legislation. At the same time, the child's attachment to the foster parents is considered important. Child welfare practice is thus influenced by different theories on biology and attachment.

From growing up with relatives to formal kinship care

In former times children often grew up with relatives without the involvement of public bodies or the notion of foster care. There were many and varied reasons for children to grow up with their kin; they varied over time but could include illness or death of parents, very young age of parents, poverty and the absence of mothers from the home because of work.

Because children in the foster care of relatives in the early years of the CWS were often considered "illegitimate", that is to say born out of wedlock, their existence was somehow shameful, and relatives could reserve the right to refuse the burden which would accompany caring for such a child. "Illegitimate" (foster) children in the family might bring social degradation, and in this respect it was the most well-to-do who had the most to lose. Of those who nevertheless still functioned as kinship carers in that period, the majority were grandmothers, followed by aunts (generally mothers' sisters). Foster care with more distant relatives hardly occurred (Andresen, 2006, pp. 90–93). When relatives, despite the social burdens it could bring, still assumed responsibility, it was often interpreted as a guarantee of good care:

> (...) When placement was imminent, relatives or acquaintances volunteered to receive the children. This circumstance is surely a guarantee that the children will be treated with care and be properly brought up.
>
> (Administrator for the poor in Bergen in 1907, quoted in Andresen, 2006, p. 90).

In the city of Bergen, the majority of foster care placements during the period 1903–1941 were with relatives (Andresen, 2006, p. 91). The name 'foster home' implied that the home received payment from the government to have the child. Relatives or others who cared for the children of others in their own family without such remuneration are therefore not included in the foster home records. As a result there is no documentation of how common it was to grow up, for example, with grandmothers or other relatives. Statistics Norway (SSB) initiated the first systematic national registration of kinship care in 1992.

The resistance of the CWS to the placement of children in their own families is documented in several studies from different countries (Knudsen & Egelund, 2011; Moldestad, 1996; Vinnerljung, 1993; Winokur, Holtan, & Valentine, 2009), and can be seen as closely linked to the influence of contemporary social scientists, as represented by the new professional groups that grew out of the welfare state in the West at the end of the 1960s. Social work was at that time constituted as a field of professional education and work in Norway. The social work approach laid the groundwork for an inter-generational perspective with the aim of preventing what Jonsson (1969) described as "social inheritance". It was presumed that neglectful parents came from neglectful homes and thereby lacked the skills to take good care of children. If the aim were to prevent a negative social inheritance being passed down to the children, placement of children in their own families should be avoided, as expressed below:

> Occasionally one is gripped by the urge to liberate these children from their social and psychological inheritance, let them break the cycle and start afresh.
>
> (Vinterhed, 1985, p. 69)

In an interview-based study of social workers, Moldestad (1996) discovered their basic belief that children who were being moved to foster care ought predominantly to live with strangers. For their own children, on the other hand, the social workers felt that the natural place to grow up would be with close family. The study illustrates the professional approach generally adopted by the children's services at the time. This resulted in a restrictive approach towards relatives as caregivers around the turn of the millennium.

Another obstacle to the placement of children with relatives was the fact that the children's services perceived that they had less power to regulate kinship care arrangements. Controlling the contact between parents and children was difficult when grandparents, aunts and uncles were responsible for organising visiting arrangements. It was feared that grandparents in the role of foster parents would experience a conflict of loyalties and conflicting pressures between the demands of their own children and those of the CWS. It would, for example, be difficult to stick to limitations on contact between birth parents and children.

A change of attitude and the formalisation of kinship care as an official intervention

Previously, unlike the situation with other types of foster care, it was frequently not the children's services (because of widespread scepticism), but the relatives themselves, in particular grandparents, who took the initiative to be approved as foster carers for their grandchildren. Many of those who wished to take on the care of a grandchild experienced having to fight for the approval of the CWS (Holtan, 2002). As in the early days of the CWS, it is still the child's grandparents and aunts and uncles, predominantly on the mother's side, who are kinship carers today. This is the case both in Norway and internationally (Broad, 2004; Cuddeback, 2004; Holtan & Thørnblad, 2009). Chapter 5 has more detailed information about this.

The incorporation of kinship care as one of the foster care interventions by the children's services was formalised in a regulation on foster care with effect from 1 January 2004. It states that: "The child welfare services shall always assess whether someone in the child's family or close networks may be chosen as foster carers" (Section 4). When the proposed new regulations on foster care which included the prioritisation of kinship care were submitted for comment, it resulted in clear support for the proposal. In 2018 these regulations were established by law.

The prioritisation of kinship care can be regarded as a result of the confluence of different circumstances. In connection with the proposed changes to the regulations in 2004, a hearing was arranged. When we investigated the attitudes to kinship placements revealed by the hearing, we found that kinship was regarded almost as a quality in itself (Thørnblad, 2009). In their statements, many contributors emphasised traditional family ideals, and that children in care ought to grow up in "normal" families. Others stressed the biological principle in the sense that biological attachment was considered particularly important for social attachment ("blood is thicker than water"). Another argument in favour of incorporating growing up with relatives as kinship care was the wish for equal treatment of everybody who takes on the role of foster parent. The milieu around the child welfare service thus supported changing the regulations to reflect the need for children's services to investigate possible foster care within the child's family and networks.

Another influence on the change in the view of kinship care was research findings which showed that both children and relatives valued this type of foster care because it constituted a type of care which was familiar to the child (Mason, Falloon, Gibbons, Spence, & Scott, 2002). Other reasoning was anchored in studies showing that children in non-kinship care too often experienced unintentional moves and lost contact with their family of origin (Einarsson & Sandbæk, 1997).

Another reason for the prioritisation of kinship care is that its aim as an intervention is to strengthen the family as an institution. In parallel with the individualisation of Western society and a care and family policy which reduces individual dependency on the family, socio-political initiatives with the aim of activating the client's family and network resources are being developed specifically in order to care for individuals. Kinship care, along with family group conferencing and other types of measures where family and network relations are included, are examples of social work approaches which in addition to giving client groups a greater degree of emancipation, aim to stimulate the distribution of responsibility and solutions in families and networks. In addition we cannot discount the possibility that the prioritisation of foster care in general and constant lack of available foster homes have contributed to a greater commitment to kinship care.[5]

In terms of values, kinship care also fits in with neo-liberal policy in that the family is given greater responsibility for dealing with needs and challenges in the private sphere. The same ideology favours the fact that greater effort from the private sphere contributes to the reduction of public spending. Internationally, the increased use of kinship care has been explained by the accompanying financial savings (Dubowitz et al., 1994; Dubowitz, Feigelman, & Zuravin, 1993; Gebel, 1996; Gleeson, 1996; Iglehart, 1994; Minkler & Roe, 1993). In Norway, economic reasons were not prominent when the regulatory changes were introduced in 2004. Our research from 2002 about children in care showed that kinship foster parents received the same expenses and compensation as non-kinship foster parents, but that they took advantage of other child welfare interventions to a lesser degree (Holtan, 2002). In a survey carried out by Vista Analyse in 2018, the same financial compensation was found for both types of foster care. However, in the interviews child welfare workers claimed that payments to kinship foster homes were lower than to non-kinship foster homes (Ekhaugen, Høgestøl, & Rasmussen, 2018).

Respect for ethnicity and cultural identity were also important for the prioritisation of kinship care in many Western countries. The focus on ethnicity has had considerable impact in Australia, Canada and the USA who recognised the importance of growing up within a familiar cultural context and considered living with one's kin particularly important for minority groups and indigenous populations. In Norway, issues linked to Sámi people and foster care placement were brought up. Norwegian legislation currently states that when choosing a foster home for each individual child, "appropriate consideration for the wish for continuity in the child's upbringing and for the child's ethnic, religious, cultural and linguistic background must be shown" (Child Welfare Act, Section 4–15). Consideration for cultural belonging and the inclusion of family and networks can both be understood as democratisation of practice, employed to meet the needs of both children and families.

Kinship care in line with the values of children's services

Child welfare legislation is built on values such as it being best for children to grow up with their biological parents (the biological principle).[6] Radical interventions such as official care orders are not to be used until less severe interventions have been tried (the principle of least intervention). A third principle is to secure a stable and predictable care environment for the child when care of the child is taken over by the CWS. And last but not least, the best interests of the child shall always be the fundamental consideration in all actions that concern children. These four principles constitute the basic guidelines in all professional assessments made by the children's services. Building on the biological principle which refers to the precedence of biology and family-based solutions, more comprehensive intervention than is required by the situation must not be undertaken, and the child must be secured a stable and predictable care situation. Kinship care as a care intervention can be said to be compatible with these ethical requirements which are laid down in the child welfare legislation.

A gradual increase in the prevalence of kinship care

The answer to the question of which care intervention best safeguards the "best interests of the child" in the case of an official care order is that, in most cases, foster care is preferable. It is also laid down in the legislation. Foster care in the child's family or networks, that is, kinship care, has been given precedence and must, in accordance with the new legislative amendment, be investigated before non-kinship care is considered.

But have the political guidelines of prioritisation of kinship care resulted in an increase in the proportion of kinship placements? There has been a certain increase in the proportion of children and young people in kinship care. At the end of 1996, 15 percent of children in the care of children's services/state custody were living in kinship care; however, this proportion did not include children in foster care as a support measure (Holtan, 2002, p. 12). Since 2003, around 20 percent of children in foster care have lived with relatives, a proportion which was relatively stable until 2012. Figure 2.1 shows the number of children in foster care, according to the type of foster home in the period 2007–2017.

Obtaining a clear overview of the development of the use of kinship care is not easy. This is largely due to a change in the foster care categories by Statistics Norway. Until 2013, Statistics Norway registered family placement (i.e. kinship care) as a separate category, but since

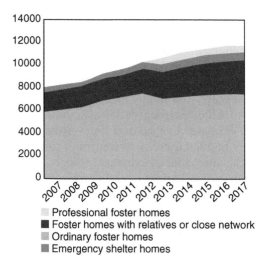

Figure 2.1 Trends in foster care between 2007 and 2017, according to the type of foster home.[7]

2013 kinship and networks are registered as one. It is reasonable to assume that the increase we have seen is partly to do with the fact that network placements are now included in the variable. At the end of 2020, 9,980 children and young people aged 0–22 lived in foster care, whereof 3,239 lived in kinship and network foster care and 6,741 in non-kinship care. The proportion of children and young people in kinship and close network foster care constituted 32.5 percent of all children aged 0–22 in foster care (SSB, 2021b).

The majority of children and young people under the age of 18 live in foster care following a decision that they should be taken into care. At the end of 2018, 85 percent of children and young people aged 0–17 were living in foster care following official care orders and 15 percent following decisions on support measures (SSB, 2021b). When children reach the age of 18, custody comes to an end, and for those who continue to live in foster care the custody arrangement is changed to a support measure.

Conclusion

In this chapter we have described different aspects of the history of the Norwegian CWS as they have been interpreted and described by historians and others. It is important to point out that this history cannot be presented as a linear development process. However, the legislative changes we have described still reflect some very clear features of the development. As pointed out by Larsen, the legislation has changed from an "ideological effort to protect society during the first phase, to family welfare in the 1950s and 1960s, parental welfare for the following 20 years, and finally to the current child-oriented perspective" (p. 206). Changes in legislation also show that the power and control of the CWS have changed over time – from an explicit control aspect to a more implicit exercise of control, facilitated through psychological insights into child development (Picot, 2014).

How we understand children, childhood and parenthood has changed radically during this period. The CWS were established in a society and a period where children without people to care for them were left to themselves or to haphazard care. In today's child-oriented society the child is an independent legal subject. The essence of parenthood and foster parenthood has changed over time from upbringing to care and in later years to a greater emphasis on supporting the child's development. A prevailing understanding in the children's services today is early intervention in order to prevent a wider need for assistance and more intrusive intervention. The CWS are expanding in the sense that a greater part of the private sphere becomes relevant to the child welfare system, such as when relatives become foster parents.

A range of professional and political currents have contributed to the current prioritisation of kinship care. Below is a brief summary of some of them:

- Increased emphasis on democratic decision-making processes, giving children and parents in the care of children's services stronger co-determination.
- Values- and faith-based interests which spoke up for strengthening family values in society, and trends which stressed the importance of biological attachment for social/psychological attachment.
- A general prioritisation of foster care over child protection institutions.
- Resource allocation for professional development in child welfare and in the recruitment of foster homes.
- Pressure from relevant private individuals (generally grandparents).

In the more recent period, juridification[8] may also have played a part, for example, through demands for equal rights for everyone who assumes the responsibility of caring for children.

These currents reflect other changes in society and make Ericsson's concept of "child welfare services as a mirror of society" just as relevant today as it was 20 years ago.

Notes

1 Children were also "put away" under the 1863 Poor Act. These were in particular orphaned or deserted children, or the children of parents who did not fulfil their duty of care or who treated those they were meant to care for in a reckless manner. The Poor Board was given responsibility for children with difficult home conditions, such as "drink" and neglect, disorder and uncleanliness (Hagen, 2001, p. 63). However, the "putting away" of children under the Poor Act did require the parents' agreement. If they refused to agree, the case would be decided by the custody committee. With the 1900 Poor Act the poor relief system came to an end (Mykland & Masdalen, 1987, p. 137).

2 Hagen (2001, p. 75) refers to NOBA no. 2, 1925 and no. 8, 1935.

3 Eilert Sundt (1817–1875) was a pioneer of sociological studies in Norway. He was a theologian and social scientist with a particular interest in working-class living conditions. Sundt's writings are available at the Central Register of Historical Data (RHD), a national institution at the University of Tromsø – The Arctic University of Norway: http://www.rhd.uit.no/sundt/sundt.html.

4 "Total institutions" denote institutions where people are isolated from the rest of society for long periods. The concept was developed by Erving Goffman in his book *Asylum*, which was based on a field study from a psychiatric hospital in the USA (Goffman, 1961).

5 The Norwegian Directorate for Children, Youth and Family Affairs has been running a project using family consultation as a method to broaden the "search field" for possible foster families, thereby increasing the recruitment of kinship and network foster care.

6 The Child Welfare Act uses the term "biological parents".

7 Figure 2.1 is from official report NOU 2018: 18 (2018, p. 50) and is published here with permission from the Ministry of Children and Families.

8 The term juridification is often used to denote the process whereby the law has come to exert an increasing influence over a greater part of society. According to Østerud, Engelstad og Selle (2003, p. 116), juridification involves giving citizens not only rights and services, but also a shift of power from democratically elected bodies to holders of legal rights and the judicial system.

References

Ainsworth, M. D. S. (1973). The development of infant-mother attachment. In B. Caldwell & H. N. Ricciuti (Eds.), *Review of Child Development Research* (pp. 1–94). Chicago, IL: University of Chicago Press.

Andresen, A. (2006). *Hender små: Bortsetting av barn i Norge 1900–1950.* Bergen, Norway: Fagbokforlaget.

Barne- likestillings- og inkluderingsdepartementet. (2016). *Trygghet og omsorg – Fosterhjem til barns beste.* (Meld. St. 17 (2015–2016)). Oslo, Norway: Departmentet.

Barne- og familiedepartementet. (2003). *FNs konvensjon om barnets rettigheter.* Vedtatt av De forente nasjoner 20. november 1989. Ratifisert av Norge 8. januar 1991. Revidert oversettelse mars 2003 med tilleggsprotokoller.

Blom, K. (2004). *Norsk barndom gjennom 150 år. En innføring.* Bergen, Norway: Fagbokforlaget.

Broad, B. (2004). Kinship care for children in the UK: Messages from research, lessons for policy and practice. *European Journal of Social Work, 7*(2), 211–227. doi:10.1080/1369145042000237463.

Börjeson, B., Magnberg, A., Nording, H., & Persson, M. (1976). *I föräldrars ställe. En studie i fosterbarnens livssituation.* Stockholm: AWE/Gebers.

Cederström, A., & Hessle, M. (1980). *Barn i kris. Yt- och djupanpassning hos fosterbarn – en teoretisk förstudie.* (Rapport nr. 50). Stockholm: Stockholms socialförvaltning, Barnbyn Skå.

Cuddeback, G. S. (2004). Kinship family foster care: A methodological and substantive synthesis of research. *Children and Youth Services Review, 26*(7), 623–639. doi:10.1016/j.childyouth.2004.01.014.

Dubowitz, H., Feigelman, S., Harrington, D., Starr, R., Zuravin, S., & Sawyer, R. (1994). Children in kinship care: How do they fare. *Children and Youth Services Review, 16*(1–2), 85–106.

Dubowitz, H., Feigelman, S., & Zuravin, S. (1993). A profile of kinship care. *Child Welfare, 72*(2), 153–169.

Einarsson, J. H., & Sandbæk, M. (1997). *Forebyggende arbeid og hjelpetiltak i barneverntjenesten. Med vekt på en myndiggjørende praksis.* (Temahefte 2/97). Oslo, Norway: NOVA.

Ekhaugen, T., Høgestøl, A., & Rasmussen, I. (2018). *Kommunenes tilbud til sine fosterhjem. Et kunnskapsgrunnlag for Fosterhjemsutvalget.* (Rapport nr. 2018/10). Oslo, Norway: Vista Analyse.

Ekhaugen, T., & Rasmussen, I. (2016). *Bruken av private aktører i barnevernet – ansvar på avveie?* (Rapport nr. 2016/19). Oslo, Norway: Vista Analyse.

Ericsson, K. (1996). *Barnevern som samfunnsspeil.* Oslo, Norway: Pax.

Ericsson, K. (2002). *Noen trekk ved barnevernets utvikling mellom 1954 og 1980. Historisk og barnevernfaglig delrapport.* Vedlegg til: Rapport fra Granskningsutvalget for barnevernsinstitusjoner, avgitt 26. juni, 2003. (Skriftserie nr. 4). Oslo, Norway: NOVA.

Gebel, T. J. (1996). Kinship care and non-relative family foster care: A comparison of caregiver attributes and attitudes. *Child Welfare, 75*(1), 5–18.

Gleeson, J. P. (1996). Kinship care as a child welfare service: The policy debate in an era of welfare reform. *Child Welfare, 75*(5), 419–449.

Goffman, E. (1961). *Asylums: Essays on the social situation of mental patients and other inmates.* Garden City, NY: Doubleday.

Goldstein, J., Freud, A., & Solnit, A. J. (1973). *Beyond the best interests of the child.* New York, NY: Free Press.

Hagen, G. (2001). *Barnevernets historie – om makt og avmakt i det 20. århundret.* Oslo, Norway: Akribe.

Hagen, G. (2004). *Norsk barnevernsamband gjennom 80 år: en beretning om de private organisasjoner i barnevernet.* Oslo, Norway: Norsk barnevernsamband.

Haugli, T. (2000). *Samværsrett i barnevernssaker.* (2. utg.). Oslo, Norway: Universitetsforlaget.

Helland, H. S., & Skivenes, M. (2019). *Adopsjon som barneverntiltak.* Bergen, Norway: Centre for Research on Discretion and Paternalism, Universitetet i Bergen.

Holtan, A. (2002). *Barndom i fosterhjem i egen slekt.* (Doktoravhandling). Universitetet i Tromsø.

Holtan, A., & Thørnblad, R. (2009). Kinship foster parenting; gender, class and labour-force participation. *European Journal of Social Work, 12*(4), 465–478. doi:10.1080/13691450902840655.

Iglehart, A. P. (1994). Kinship foster care: Placement, service, and outcome issues. *Children and Youth Services Review, 16*(1–2), 107–122. doi:10.1016/0190-7409(94)90018-3

Ingvaldsen, S. (2001). Rette foreldre og virkelige barn. Norsk adopsjonslovgivning 1917–1986. *Historisk Tidsskrift, 80*(1), 3–28.

Jon, N. (2007). *En skikkelig gutt. Arbeidet med å forme en passende maskulinitet på Foldin verneskole 1953–1970.* Oslo, Norway: Unipub.

Jonsson, G. (1969). *Det sociala arvet.* Stockholm: Tidens Förlag

Knudsen, L., & Egelund, T. (2011). *Effekter af slægtspleje. Slægtsanbragte børn og unges udvikling sammenlignet med plejebørn fra traditionelle plejefamilier.* (Rapport nr. 11:20). København, Denmark: SFI.

Larsen, G. (2002). *Barnevern i hundre år: Et overblikk på lovreformhistorien.* Oslo, Norway: Institutt for kriminologi og rettssosiologi, avdeling for kriminologi, UiO.

Mason, J., Falloon, J., Gibbons, L., Spence, N., & Scott, E. (2002). *Understanding Kinship care.* Haymarked NSW, Australia: NSW Association of Children's Welfare Agencies Inc. University of Western Sydney.

Midré, G. (1990). *Bot, bedring eller brød? Om bedømming og behandling av sosial nød fra reformasjonen til folketrygden.* Oslo, Norway: Universitetsforlaget.

Minkler, M., & Roe, K. M. (1993). *Grandmothers as caregivers: Raising children of the crack cocaine epidemic.* Newbury Park, CA: Sage.

Moldestad, B. (1996). *Egne barn – andres unger? En undersøkelse om sosialarbeideres mening om fosterbarns familie som plasseringssted.* (Hovedoppgave i sosialt arbeid). Norges teknisk-naturvitenskapelige universitet (NTNU).

Mykland, L., & Masdalen, K.-O. (1987). *Administrasjonshistorie og arkivkunnskap: kommunene.* Oslo, Norway: Universitetsforlaget.

NOU 2000: 12. (2000). *Barnevernet i Norge – Tilstandsvurderinger, nye perspektiver og forslag til reformer.* Oslo, Norway: Barne- og likestillings departementet

NOU 2016: 16. (2016). *Ny barnevernslov – Sikring av barnets rett til omsorg og beskyttelse.* Oslo, Norway: Barne- og likestillingsdepartementet.

Pettersen, K.-S. (2005). *Tatere og misjonen. Mangfold, makt og motstand.* (Doktoravhandling). Norges teknisk-naturvitenskapelige universitet (NTNU). (NOVA Rapport nr. 2/05). Oslo, Norway: NOVA.

38   *Kinship care in a historical context*

Picot, A. (2014). Transforming child welfare: From explicit to implicit control of families. *European Journal of Social Work, 17*(5), 689–701. doi:10.1080/13 691457.2014.932273.

Seip, A. L. (1994a). *Sosialhjelpstaten blir til: Norsk sosialpolitikk 1740–1920.* (2. utg.). Oslo, Norway: Gyldendal.

Seip, A. L. (1994b). *Veiene til velferdsstaten: Norsk sosialpolitikk 1920–75.* Oslo, Norway: Gyldendal.

Simonsen, E., & Ericsson, K. (2005). *Krigsbarn i fredstid.* Oslo, Norway: Universitetsforlaget.

Sköld, J. (2011). Den annorlunda normala familjen: Krav på fosterföräldrar under hundre år. In H. Bergman, M. Eriksson, & R. Klinth (Eds.), *Föräldraskapets politik – från 1900- till 2000-tal* (pp. 55–84). Stockholm: Dialogos Förlag.

Stang Dahl, T. (1978). *Barnevern og samfunnsvern: Om stat, vitenskap og profesjoner under barnevernets oppkomst i Norge.* Oslo, Norway: Pax.

Statistics Norway/Statistisk sentralbyrå (SSB). (2021a). *Adopsjoner, 2020.* (Tabell 1: Adopsjoner etter tid og adopsjonstype). Retrieved from https://www. ssb.no/befolkning/statistikker/adopsjon/aar.

Statistics Norway/Statistisk sentralbyrå (SSB). (2021b). *Barnevern, 2020.* (Tabell 5: Barnevernstiltak per 31. desember etter tiltak). Retrieved from https://www.ssb.no/barneverng/.

Sundt, E. (1870). *Om fattigforholdene i Christiania.* Christiania: J. Chr. Gundersens Bogtrykkeri.

Thuen, H. (2002). *I foreldrenes sted: Barneredningens oppdragelsesdiskurs 1820–1900. Eksempelet Toftes Gave.* Oslo, Norway: Pax.

Thørnblad, R. (2009). Slektsfosterhjem i offentlig barnevern [Kinship care in child welfare]. *Tidsskriftet Norges Barnevern, 86*(4), 221–235.

Vinnerljung, B. (1993). Släktingplaceringar i fosterbarnsvården. *Socionomens Forskningssupplement, 6*, 3–10.

Vinterhed, K. (1985). *De andra föräldrarna: om fosterföräldrars förållningssätt till fosterbarn.* Stockholm: Skeab.

Weihe, H. J. (2004). *Sosialt arbeid – historie og bakgrunn.* Oslo, Norway: Gyldendal.

Winokur, M., Holtan, A., & Valentine, D. (2009). Kinship care for the safety, permanency, and well-being of children removed from the home for maltreatment. *Cochrane Database of Systematic Reviews, Issue 1. Art. No.: CD006546.* Retrieved from http://db.c2admin.org/doc-pdf/Winokur_Kinshipcare_review.pdf. doi:10.1002/14651858.CD006546.pub2.

Østerud, Ø., Engelstad, F., & Selle, P. (2003). *Makten og demokratiet. En sluttbok fra Makt- og demokratiutredningen.* Oslo, Norway: Gyldendal Akademisk.

3   Kinship care in research

Results, limitations and
alternatives

Kinship care, from a risk to a resource

The research on kinship care which emerged in the USA in the 1990s
followed on from the marked increase in the number of children who
grew up in kinship care. US child protection agencies, like those
in Norway, had until then sought to avoid kinship placements. Researchers from the USA have partly linked the resistance to relatives
as foster parents to the theory of generational abuse (Jackson, 1999).
From this perspective, parental neglect is understood as a result of the
parents themselves having experienced abuse. Placing children with
their grandparents is therefore regarded as undesirable. As described
in Chapter 2, this scepticism has been linked to perspectives on negative social inheritance, perspectives which emerged in the Nordic
countries in the 1960s. There are several similarities between the two
theories; however, the theory of social inheritance can be interpreted
as being the more comprehensive in that it embraces socio-economic
considerations.

The increase in the number of kinship placements in the USA can
be traced to several factors, including a great need for foster care for
children who were unable to live with their parents, the reduction in
the number of available foster homes and economic considerations[1]
(Cuddeback, 2004). Increased weighting of children's contact with
their immediate family and other relatives was another central reason
for the change in the status of kinship care internationally. The influential organisation the Child Welfare League of America (CWLA)
maintained that kinship care could guarantee that children would
grow up with people whom they knew and trusted, and that this could
reduce any possible trauma linked to moving in with "strangers". It
was further argued that growing up in kinship care gave children the
opportunity to maintain their social and familial networks and their

DOI: 10.4324/9781003231363-3

cultural identity to a greater extent. The thinking was then, and still is, that growing up in kinship care can contribute to creating security and continuity in the lives of children, and thus also to a better childhood (Child Welfare League of America, 1994). The same reasons have by varying degrees also been central to the legitimisation of kinship care in Norway, where today relatives are formally promoted as a resource rather than a risk (cf. Chapter 2).

The assumption that kinship care could guarantee that children were able to maintain their cultural identity was an important reason for the change in the status of kinship care internationally. The new emphasis can be understood as part of a move by public agencies against discriminating practices towards minorities and indigenous peoples. In Australia, for example, the child welfare authorities had almost exclusively placed Aboriginal children in the majority population. Much like in other countries, where indigenous populations had experienced years of suppression and assimilation, the increased attention on kinship foster placements was an attempt to do something about the expressed concerns for their children voiced by Aboriginal communities. According to reports, their experience was of 'their' children being stolen from the communities to which they belonged and robbed of their cultural belonging and identity (Yardley, Mason, & Watson, 2009).

A need for evidence

Research contributions from the USA in the early 1990s reflect the controversy caused by the increase in the number of kinship foster placements. At a time when evidence-based practice[2] had begun to become a slogan in the USA, the number of kinship placements increased without any research-based knowledge of the effects of the initiative (Berrick, Barth & Needell, 1994).

The arguments put forward in favour of kinship care were, in other words, not based on research-based knowledge, but on theories and values. It was therefore not possible to know whether the preference for kinship care over non-kinship care actually had evidence-based legitimacy. Counter-arguments, similar to the scepticism of kinship care which had previously been dominant in child protection services, were also raised by critical voices. The criticism was in particular directed towards grandparents. Questions were asked whether the same individuals who had raised deviant members of society should be given a second chance (Goerge, Wulczyn, & Fanshel, 1994). Gradually, as research results showed that kinship foster parents had a greater chance of forming single-person households and with poorer health and lower income compared to non-kinship foster parents, they were also drawn into the debate about the quality of kinship care (Bartholet, 1999; Pierce, 1999) (see also Chapter 5). Despite strong views from various quarters, little was known about how these children were actually doing (Dubowitz et al., 1994), and the need for research with a higher level of evidence about the effects of kinship care was emphasised as one of the most important areas of future research (Goerge et al., 1994; Iglehart, 1994).

Just over a decade later, the knowledge status of kinship care was summarised as follows:

> The existing research tends to focus on the demographic characteristics of children in kinship care, the characteristics of kinship carers and the provision of services. There is limited research examining the effectiveness and outcomes of kinship care for children.
>
> (Paxman, 2006, p. 1)

Paxman's literature review shows that there were studies investigating the effects of kinship care compared with non-kinship care at the time. However, as seen in the quotation above, they were in a minority compared to descriptive studies. Furthermore, there were considerable methodological challenges among the actual available studies, such as small samples and where the comparison groups were also not controlled. So, despite an increase in the volume of research on outcomes of kinship care compared to non-kinship care, this research could not show which type of foster care was in the child's best interest.

It was during this period (late 1990s) that we embarked on our research project, which was first and foremost a qualitative study of children's social integration, with particular emphasis on family belonging. We also recognised the need to identify significant factors pertaining to kinship care. As previously mentioned, there was no Norwegian research on kinship care, and we carried out a descriptive study which compared kinship care with non-kinship care in terms of stability, patterns of parent-child interaction, child protection history, socio-economic status of foster parents and what kind of official support the homes received (Holtan, 2002). By including data based on standardised measuring instruments such as the Child Behaviour Checklist, we compared the mental health of children in kinship care with the mental health of children in non-kinship care, a study which may be characterised as a type of impact research (Holtan, Rønning,

Handegård, & Sourander, 2005). When we collected new data on the children's mental health seven to eight years later (T2), we studied the development of the children's mental health longitudinally (Vis, Handegård, Holtan, Fossum, & Thørnblad, 2014). We also studied the stability of kinship care and non-kinship care over a period of time (Holtan, Handegård, Thørnblad & Vis, 2013). In the following sections we provide a brief summary of the findings from this research.

The impact of kinship care

In order to meet the requirement for more trusted evidence, Winokur, Holtan and Valentine carried out a systematic review along the lines of the Campbell and Cochrane collaborations, which was published in 2009. In all, 62 quasi-experimental studies were included. In 2014, Winokur, Holtan and Batchelder published an updated version which included 102 quasi-experimental studies. The majority of these studies are from the USA (89); however, Australia (4), the Netherlands (2), Spain (2), Norway (1), Sweden (1), Ireland (1), UK and Israel (1) are also represented. The number does not show the actual volume of studies comparing outcomes of kinship care with non-kinship care, but rather the number of studies which fulfilled the inclusion criteria stipulated for the analysis in the systematic review. The total number of studies was therefore higher.[3] Even if we only look at the studies which fulfilled the criteria, the number from 2014 reflects a considerable increase from the number included in 2009. It is still worth mentioning that only two of the studies are from the Nordic countries. Let us now take a closer look at the results of this research, using the most recently published review as our starting point.

Campbell/Cochrane reviews have two objectives: to undertake the most thorough, objective and scientifically based compilation possible of all the available research literature in the field, and to seek to provide the best possible answer to whether a particular intervention works, based on explicit criteria. The primary outcome measures in the report of Winokur, Holtan and Batchelder (2014) included the behavioural development and mental health of children and young people under the age of 18, as well as the placement stability and permanence in the care situation. Secondary outcome measures were educational level, family relations, the use of services and post-placement abuse.

- Behavioural development was measured using standardised instruments such as the Child Behaviour Checklist (CBCL), reports by caregivers, teachers and/or the children. The analysis of data using these measures showed that children in non-kinship foster homes had a 1.6 times greater chance of behavioural problems compared to children in kinship care. Our results based on the analysis of data from T1 showed a similar result. (Holtan, Rønning, Handegård, & Sourander, 2005). This study is included in the research review.

- Shortly after Winokur's updated systematic review, we published our follow-up study after eight years (Vis et al., 2014). The study was based on data from T1 and T2 which reported the occurrence and changes over time of emotional and behavioural problems in 233 young people who had lived in foster homes, both in kinship care and in non-kinship care. There was no change in the mean problem score from T1 to T2; however, there were granular changes. The changes are partly explained by gender. Girls experienced more problems, while boys experienced fewer. Kinship foster homes appear to have provided protection against mental difficulties during the childhood years (in T1), but did not appear to be a factor in the incidence of mental problems during the teenage years. Living in a foster home in the same municipality as before the foster care placement was associated with fewer problems in both the childhood and teenage years.

- In the review, mental health was measured using standardised instruments, reports from care givers, reports from teachers and self-reporting. The analysis of the outcome measures, which included both psychiatric illness and well-being, showed that children in non-kinship foster homes had a two times greater chance of having mental illness compared with children in kinship care. Children in kinship care had a two times greater chance of reported well-being compared with children in non-kinship foster homes.

- Stability: The stability criteria in the review were the number of placements, placement breakdown (unintended moves), placement duration and re-placement. They were measured using secondary data from the administrative databases of the CWS. Children in non-kinship foster homes had a 1.9 times greater chance of placement breakdown and a 2.6 times greater chance of three or more placements compared with children in kinship care. There was no significant difference in placement duration and total placement length during care between kinship and non-kinship care. At this point we would like to add results from our study of breakdown in long-term foster home placements in Norway based on data from T1 and T2. Unlike the systematic review, we found no difference between kinship and non-kinship care as far as stability at T2 was concerned. The children who did experience placement breakdown had on average lived almost nine years in the foster home (Holtan et al., 2013). The findings indicate that when children have lived for several years in non-kinship foster homes, the relationship between children and foster parents does become closer. In other words, over time, non-kinship foster families acquire some of the characteristics which constitute the starting point of many kinship foster homes, such as closeness, relatedness and commitment. The study was published after Winokur had completed the data collection, and our study is not included in the Campbell/Cochrane review.

• Permanency: Reunification, adoption, guardianship and continued care were measured using data from administrative databases as well as on the basis of records from the CWS, schools and health services. There was no difference in return to the birth parents. Children in non-kinship care had a 2.5 times greater chance of being adopted compared with children in kinship care. Children in kinship situations had a 3.8 greater chance of remaining under guardianship and a 1.2 greater chance of remaining in care compared with children in non-kinship foster homes. Because different countries have different policies, the significance of these findings will vary.[4] In the USA, adoption is a desired outcome, and placements lasting more than 12 months are considered detrimental to children. In Norway, on the other hand, we favour long-term placements over adoption.

• Secondary outcome measures: There was no difference in the education level or in family relationships (conflict, family functioning) between children in kinship care and children in non-kinship care. Children in non-kinship care had a 2.4 times greater chance of receiving support from psychiatric health care and a 3.7 times greater chance of abuse by foster parent(s) compared to children in kinship care.[5]

In summary, the systematic review shows that children in kinship care had a lower incidence of behavioural problems and psychiatric conditions, more stable placements, lower levels of adoption and higher incidence of being placed under guardianship as compared with children in non-kinship care.

As already mentioned, there was no difference in reunification, that is to say whether children moved back to their birth parents. The study further showed that children and foster parents in kinship care received fewer services compared with children in non-kinship care. Based on the definition of the variables in the study, there was no difference in educational level and family relationship. The conclusion, based on these findings, is therefore that kinship care is a viable alternative for CWS to consider when children for various reasons cannot live with their parents.

The findings from the study can be read as the best available evidence of the effects of kinship care. As pointed out by Winokur and colleagues, the results do not mean that kinship care is the right solution in every case of a child being placed outside the home. The choice of foster care must have each individual child as its starting point. The systematic review by Winokur, Holtan and Batchelder has nevertheless been important for legitimising kinship care as a standard measure for CWS. At the same time, the impact studies may have had a positive significance for families who wish to become foster parents to children of their own kin, in their encounters with the CWS. The studies nevertheless present many challenges which are significant for the interpretation and practical use of the findings. These are described and discussed below.

Methodological challenges

The criticism aimed at studies of the effects of kinship care has focused on methodological limitations. Important questions have been raised about whether one would have arrived at the same answers if the measurement had been carried out several times (reliability), and about whether what is actually measured is what was intended to be measured (validity).

The measurement of impact is generally graded by level of evidence, with randomised controlled trials (RCT) defined as the highest level. There are no randomised controlled trials in foster home studies. That would require selecting the type of foster home for the child randomly, something which is ethically impossible to do. As mentioned above, we are therefore dealing with quasi-experimental studies.[6]

However, if we move away from randomisation as the governing principles, it is the quality of the actual studies we need to discuss. Winokur, Holtan and Batchelder (2014) assessed their study against several quality indicators (p. 6), and concluded that the highest risk of bias was in terms of *selection* and the lowest in terms of *reporting*.[7] In other words, there was uncertainty or a high risk of the children being different in terms of physical and mental health, their history in the child welfare system and age at the time of moving to the foster home, and a low risk of the results having been communicated differently. This means that the results must be approached with some caution since there is insufficient knowledge to be able to ascertain whether it is the actual type of foster home (kinship versus non-kinship) that is the reason for the positive findings of kinship care. Given that the studies to a large degree concur as far as positive results for kinship care are concerned, we can nevertheless presume that they are linked to the qualities of kinship care.

What has happened in the field of research since Winokur and colleagues published their systematic reviews? Searches on kinship care in the literature indicate that research comparing kinship care with non-kinship care constitutes the majority of the studies published after 2014. The studies attempt in various ways to evaluate the impact and outcomes of placements.

When we look more closely at these studies, we see that methodological weaknesses are often given as reasons for the importance of continued study of the effects of kinship care (see for example Andersen & Fallesen, 2015; Bergström et al., 2019; Denby, Testa, Alford, Chad, & Brinson, 2017; Font, 2014). We see an example of this in the article "Is Higher Placement Stability in Kinship Care By Virtue or Design?" by Font (2015). The title is a direct reference to the current research which shows a higher degree of stability in kinship care as compared with non-kinship care. Font's study shows similar results. However, the questions she poses are not whether kinship care is more stable, but what makes them more stable compared to non-kinship care and on what conditions. Based on her comprehensive analysis of data from administrative databases in Wisconsin, USA, from 2005 to 2012, Font argues that the reason for this stability is to a large extent the children themselves. In other words, the children who grow up in the foster care of their own kin have fewer mental and physical conditions before the foster care placement is formalised, and thus a better starting point than children in non-kinship care. As such she takes into account one of the weaknesses exposed by Winokur, Holtan and Batchelder (2014) concerning a high risk of bias in the selection.

Transferability to practice

In his contribution to the debate about evidence-based practice, Frost (2002, p. 43) uses kinship care as an example to point out the limitations of transferring results from impact studies to practice. Frost points out that even if children and young people who grow up in kinship care score "higher" in impact studies, we cannot necessarily predict that all kinship placements will be successful. Neither can the findings be transferred to direct practice with the individual child (McCarthy & Edwards, 2011, p. 68), which again means that it is difficult for practitioners to actually use this knowledge. The findings are better suited to policy formation, as we have seen in the case of changes in the regulations and legislation for kinship care (Chapter 2). These state that kinship placement should always be considered, but the consideration of the best interest of each individual child is the decisive factor in the choice of foster care.

Despite the difficulty in transferring this research to the practice level, there is a demand for additional meta studies which analyse all available research, and which accommodate the methodological weaknesses – research which can provide us with information on the impact of kinship care. This implies an understanding of the existence of a universal "truth" about kinship care which can be captured and measured.

Reproduction of the child welfare services understandings

From the above perspective, questions are rarely asked about the construction of the research object (Bourdieu & Wacquant, 1992), that is, which preconceptions the research is based on and how growing up in kinship care is understood and studied? In impact research, kinship care is primarily studied as an intervention. The intervention construction represents the preconstructed understanding of kinship care as an intervention, one that is anchored in the field of child welfare. This leads to questions of the impact, risk, advantages and disadvantages of the intervention, and we find it more or less instinctive to compare kinship care with non-kinship care. One risk of this is that the research reproduces the preconceptions, issues, theories and logic of the CWS, and so does not yield new knowledge which is independent of the child welfare system.

The technologisation of kinship care

According to Ulvik, the intervention construction is technological and analogous to biomedical research; "it is the effect of the pill which is being studied" (2009, pp. 21–22). The challenge is that kinship care is not a technology, but a category comprising a multitude of family types and relationships. Variation in family life can be seen from several angles. For example, some children grow up with their grandparents; others with their uncle or aunt or other relatives. The relatives who function as foster parents are in some cases single, while others are married or co-habiting. There is also a great difference in how often the children have contact with their parents, from several times a week to a few times a year, or less. If we put these, and other, variations together, we see that the families in the kinship care category have many similar characteristics to other families in society today, from divorced families to nuclear families and families of adoption. At the same time, it should be said that socio-economic status as well as the presence of children's services may vary a great deal from one family to the next. It is important to be aware of variation because it supports the fact that "kinship care" is not one thing, or a bounded measure. This aspect may get lost in impact studies where one attempts to measure kinship care against non-kinship care, which of course is also not one thing. It may seem odd that the impact research almost exclusively compares kinship care with non-kinship care. As mentioned above, the answer is found in the construction of the research object. When we approach kinship care as an intervention, it becomes more or less evident to compare it with other child welfare placements. Another group with whom the kinship foster families could be compared is divorced families, where the parties are divided between different households which children to a greater or lesser extent move between.

Here we would like to add that the reasons why so much research is limited in the choice of perspectives and problems for discussion lie with who is funding the research and the proximity of the research environment to the child welfare field. Child welfare research is a relatively new field in Norway emerging in the 1980s. It is characterised by small projects, many of them carried out by Masters and PhD students in child welfare and social work education. Much of the remaining research is carried out at the request of the Norwegian Directorate for Children, Youth and Family Affairs (Bufdir). This usually implies time-limited, small projects which provide answers to concrete issues, often confined to the current paradigm of the CWS.

Actors in the shaping of family life

The acknowledgement that kinship care consists of a wide variety of family types and relationships implies an understanding that studies into kinship care solely as an intervention will represent a reductionist approach to the phenomenon. The complexity is also exposed by the fact that children and adults may have different understandings or definitions of their family as an ordinary family, extended family, grandparent family or foster family. Such understandings may change over time. This is in accordance with the current sociological under-standings of family life and relations, which emphasise the importance of studying family as an activity rather than a static unit assigned through biology (see Chapter 6 for a more detailed description). Different descriptions of who belong to one's family are illustrated in the study by Castrén and Widmer (2015) of families after separa-tion and re-partnering. The study shows that who is inside and who is outside one person's definition of family can vary from one family member to the next. However, the study also exemplifies another im-portant point, namely that children are active actors in the construc-tion of family. This is also apparent in other studies, where children are asked to describe what being a family actually means, and who they themselves would include as members of it (Davies, 2013; Gil-lies, McCarthy, & Holland, 2001). These studies show that children and young people understand family to mean supporting one another, being there for one another and living and spending time together. The studies further show that children and young people include as family members individuals who give them a feeling of belonging and safety. This is not an indication that children necessarily exclude diffi-cult relationships in the definition of family. However, what the studies show is that questions around family are not determined only by biol-ogy, but by the relationships and activities that individuals – children as well as adults – are part of, what they "do" in their everyday life. The impact research does not include the family understandings of children and adults, that is to say what kinship care means to them. Neither is children as actors considered. When studying the effects of foster care placements on children, it may be taken for granted that children are passive recipients of care, and that the outcome is a result of the care or lack of care which has been given. Not only does that lead to the importance of children's participation in their own lives disappearing, but the foster parents may be reduced to "suppliers" of care. The dynamic aspect of the everyday life of children and adults may thus simply expire and be replaced by a static approach.

The importance of context

Another important perspective is the social and cultural contexts in which family life is lived and practised. Like the category 'kinship care', childhood, parenthood and family are not static. How the various cat-egories are described and understood changes both in and between societies and cultures over time. Children who grow up in Norway may have different understandings of what childhood is or should be, compared with children growing up in other countries. Growing up as a "foster child" with, for example, a grandmother may have different meanings among children and adults not only in different countries, but also in the same country.

Ignoring social and cultural contexts becomes particularly problematic when attempting to generalise findings around kinship care across borders, as is done in reviews of current knowledge. The analysis of Winokur, Holtan and Batchelder (2014) also tries to communicate something about a more or less universal category. But even if we acknowledge that there are similarities within the category, it does not mean that the similarity plays out in the same way. One example is socio-economic resources. As we also point out in other chapters, a number of studies show that foster parents in kinship foster homes have a greater chance of having fewer socio-economic resources available than non-kinship foster parents. However, the consequences of having fewer socio-economic resources available in Norway, with our type of welfare state, will be different to those in other countries, for example, the USA and the UK. Another significant factor is that the legislation and regulations of the CWS vary greatly from country to country, including in the Nordic countries. This means that the guidelines and support which come with the formalisation of foster home initiatives give the families different opportunities and limitations in different countries. In other words, kinship care is not a universal category. What it consists of will vary both in and between countries.

Growing up with relatives, an alternative research approach

So far, we have described results and highlighted challenges of the impact research into kinship care. The next task is to determine which alternative approaches will enable us to limit or overcome these challenges. One possible alternative is to study kinship care as "growing up with relatives" – as family. This implies acknowledging that kinship care is not one thing, but rather a category consisting of a number of different family types and relationships, and that these are practised in different social and cultural contexts. This perspective gives us the opportunity to pose different questions from those of the intervention research. This is not the same as ignoring the intervention aspect of kinship care. On the contrary, the construction enables us to investigate the formal aspect as a framework within which family life and relationships are practised and negotiated. Kinship care is, in other words, in itself a context which regulates and structures family life and relations.

Through the formalisation of kinship care, children are given the status of foster children, grandmother becomes foster mother, and home becomes a foster home. This leads us to ask how these frameworks impact the daily lives of people, both in the short and in the long term, and the question is turned on its head: from whether foster parents fulfil the aims and demands set by the CWS, to how the guidelines and regulations influence the understanding of childhood, parenthood and family. These questions will be looked at in the following chapters.

Conclusion

The central theme of this chapter has been research into the impact of kinship care. As described above, the existing research shows that children who grow up in kinship care manage just as well and often better than children growing up in non-kinship care. However, as has been pointed out by a number of researchers, there are many methodological challenges in the interpretation of the results of this research.

We have challenged the idea that it is possible to find an "absolute truth" about kinship care. The challenges that have been put forward here should not be interpreted as arguments that impact research is not important, useful or necessary. The CWS have an ethical responsibility to ensure that the interventions have a positive outcome. An official care order is a powerful intervention in a child's life and of great significance for children and the families themselves. It is the responsibility of the CWS to place the child in the kind of care initiative which to the greatest possible degree safeguards the child's security, stability and caring environment. As studies of kinship care have shown, impact research has been useful in terms of challenging established notions of what is in the best interest of children, and through that also to legitimise changing practice in the CWS.

That said, it should also be stated that the problem arises when kinship care is studied almost exclusively from the established perspectives of the CWS, namely as an intervention. One of the unintended consequences of this is that only one picture is presented of kinship care. It is therefore reasonable to argue in favour of additional approaches and perspectives in future studies of kinship care, for example, studies which approach kinship care as family, as we do in this book.

Finally, we want to state the need for interdisciplinary projects with a wider range of issues for discussion which not only ask questions about different impacts but also challenge the given perceptions in both research and practice fields, examples of which we have given in this chapter. We call for longitudinal studies which follow children and families over time, and which include children who grow up in different conditions. We need diversity of perspectives, perspectives which safeguard context and which are anchored outside the field of the CWS.

Notes

1 Earlier American studies showed that several kinship foster homes received less support than non-kinship care, something which also made such placements cheaper (see for example Berrick, Barth & Needell, 1994).
2 The notion of 'evidence' is not unambiguous, and is defined, used and understood in different ways within different contexts and fields. Directly translated from English, the Norwegian term for "evidence" is "bevis"; however, in the field of health and social sciences the term "best available knowledge" is more appropriate.
3 The search yielded 9,643 hits. Of these, 389 studies were found to be relevant and reviewed. 102 of the studies met the criteria for the analysis.
4 Guardianship is a frequently used arrangement in the USA as an alternative to adoption or return to the parents.
5 Based on analysis of three studies, all from the USA.
6 In a quasi-experimental design, two intervention groups are compared, but without random assignment.
7 *Selection bias*: Was group assignment determined randomly or might it have been related to outcomes or the interventions received? *Reporting bias*: Were the outcomes, measures and analyses selected a priori and reported completely? Were participants biased in their recall or response? (Winokur et al., 2014, p. 6).

References

Andersen, S. H., & Fallesen, P. (2015). Family matters? The effect of kinship care on foster care disruption rates. *Child Abuse & Neglect, 48*, 68–79. doi:10.1016/j.chiabu.2015.06.005.

Bartholet, E. (1999). *Nobody's children: Abuse and neglect, foster drift, and the adoption alternative*. Boston, MA: Beacon Press.

Bergström, M., Cederblad, M., Håkansson, K., Jonsson, A. K., Munthe, C., Vinnerljung, B., ... Sundell, K. (2019). Interventions in foster family care: a systematic review. *Research on Social Work Practice*. doi:10.1177/1049731519832101.

Berrick, J. D., Barth, R. P., & Needell, B. (1994). A comparison of kinship foster homes and foster family homes: Implications for kinship foster care as family preservation. *Children and Youth Services Review, 16*(1–2), 33–63. doi:10.1016/0190-7409(94)90015-9.

Bourdieu, P., & Wacquant, L. J. D. (1992). *An invitation to reflexive sociology.* Chicago, IL: Chicago University Press.

Castrén, A. M., & Widmer, E. D. (2015). Insiders and outsiders in stepfamilies: Adults' and children's views on family boundaries. *Current sociology,* *63*(1), 35–56. doi:10.1177/0011392114551650.

Child Welfare League of America. (1994). *Kinship care: A natural bridge.* Washington, DC: Child Welfare League of America.

Cuddeback, G. S. (2004). Kinship family foster care: A methodological and substantive synthesis of research. *Children and Youth Services Review,* *26*(7), 623–639. doi:10.1016/j.childyouth.2004.01.014.

Davies, H. (2013). Children and family transitions: Family togetherness and family contact. In J. R. McCarthy, C. A. Hooper, & V. Gillies (Eds.), *Family troubles? Exploring changes and challenges in the family lives of children and young people* (pp. 185–193). Bristol, England: Policy Press.

Denby, R. W., Testa, M. F., Alford, K. A., Chad, L., & Brinson, J. A. (2017). Protective factors as mediators and moderators of risk effects on perceptions of child well-being in kinship care. *Child Welfare,* *95*(4), 111–136.

Dubowitz, H., Feigelman, S., Harrington, D., Starr, R., Zuravin, S., & Sawyer, R. (1994). Children in kinship care: How do they fare. *Children and Youth Services Review,* *16*(1–2), 85–106.

Font, S. A. (2014). Kinship and nonrelative foster care: The effect of placement type on child well-being. *Child Development,* *85*(5), 2074–2090. doi:10.1111/cdev.12241.

Font, S. A. (2015). Is higher placement stability in kinship foster care by virtue or design?. *Child Abuse & Neglect,* *42*, 99–111. doi:10.1111/cdev.12241.

Frost, N. (2002). A problematic relationship? Evidence and practice in the workplace. *Social Work & Social Sciences Review,* *10*(1), 38–50.

Gillies, V., McCarthy, J. R., & Holland, J. (2001). *Pulling together, pulling apart: The family lives of young people aged 16–18.* London, England: Family Policy Studies Centre/Joseph Rowntree Foundation.

Goerge, R., Wulczyn, F., & Fanshel, D. (1994). A foster care research agenda for the '90s. *Child Welfare,* *73*(5), 525–549.

Holtan, A. (2002). Barndom i fosterhjem i egen slekt. (Doctoral dissertation). University of Tromsø, Norway.

Holtan, A., Handegård, B. H., Thørnblad, R., & Vis, S.A. (2013). Placement disruption in long long-lasting kinship and nonkinship foster care. *Children-and-Youth-Services-Review,* *35*(7), 1087–1094.

Holtan, A., Rønning, J. A., Handegård, B. H., & Sourander, A. (2005). A comparison of mental health problems in kinship and nonkinship foster care. *European Child & Adolescent Psychiatry,* *14*(4), 200–207. doi:10.1007/s00787-005-0445-z.

Iglehart, A. P. (1994). Kinship foster care: Placement, service, and outcome issues. *Children and Youth Services Review,* *16*(1–2), 107–122. doi:10.1016/0190-7409(94)90018-3.

Jackson, S. M. (1999). Paradigm shift: training staff to provide services to the kinship triad. In R. L. Hegar & M. Scannapieco (Eds.), *Kinship foster care. Policy, practice and research* (pp. 93–111). New York, NY: Oxford Unviersity Press.

McCarthy, J. R., & Edwards, R. (2011). *Key concepts in family studies*. London, England: Sage.

Paxman, M. (2006). Outcomes for children and young people in kinship care: an issues paper. Centre for Parenting & Research, Sydney, Australia: NSW Department of Community Services.

Pierce, W. L. (1999). Kinship care. In national council for adoption. In C. Marshner & W. L. Pierce (Eds.), *Adoption factbook III* (pp. 104–116). Waite Park, MN: Park Press Quality Printing.

Ulvik, O. S. (2009). Kunnskap for et seinmoderne barnevern: Forholdet mellom forskning og praksis. *Tidsskrift for Norges Barnevern, 86*(1), 18–27.

Vis, S. A., Handegård, B. H., Holtan, A., Fossum, S., & Thørnblad, R. (2014). Social functioning and mental health among children who have been living in kinship and non-kinship foster care: Results from an 8-year follow-up with a Norwegian sample. *Child & Family Social Work, 21*, 557–567. doi:10.1111/cfs.12180.

Winokur, M., Holtan, A., & Batchelder, K. E. (2014). Kinship care for the safety, permanency, and well-being of children removed from the home for maltreatment. *Cochrane Database of Systematic Reviews, Issue 1. Art. No.: CD006546.* doi:10.1002/14651858.CD006546.pub3.

Winokur, M., Holtan, A., & Valentine, D. (2009). Kinship care for the safety, permanency, and well-being of children removed from the home for maltreatment. *Cochrane Database of Systematic Reviews, Issue 1. Art. No.: CD006546.* Retrieved from http://db.c2admin.org/doc-pdf/Winokur_Kinshipcare_review.pdf. doi:10.1002/14651858.CD006546.pub2.

Yardley, A., Mason, J., & Watson, E. (2009). *Kinship care in NSW – finding a way forward*. Sydney, Australia: University of Western Sydney.

4 Family life in the intersection between the public and private

A formal framework around private family relationships

Formal agreements and regulations between a foster family and the CWS vary from one country to the next. In Norway, becoming formalised as a foster family, both kinship and non-kinship, is done by entering into a contract between the CWS and foster parents. The foster care contract implies that relatives become foster parents who are being given the task by the CWS to care for a relative. As foster parents, the relatives become part of the CWS in the sense that they get financial compensation, training and access to special interest groups – in principle on the same level as non-kinship foster parents.

Unlike what is generally the case in non-kinship care, kinship care is mostly based on established relationships between the relatives, and the child and the child's mother and/or father. The foster parents have not shown a general interest in becoming foster parents, but have chosen to assume the care of a particular child. In this way, children who live in kinship care are not removed from their family network like in most non-kinship placements, but are placed with people to whom they are related. The similarity with non-kinship care, however, is that CWS have approved or taken over the formal custody, which allows them to regulate and control family relationships and practices. The rights and responsibilities of kinship foster families are regulated in accordance with the same provisions as for non-kinship care.

What are the consequences of someone in the child's family entering into a foster care agreement? One consequence of the contractual relationship is that the latitude of the foster parents can be regulated or limited in line with the professional judgement of the CWS. For example, grandparents who are foster parents may be ordered to have restricted contact with their own children, that is to say the (foster) child's mother or father. Becoming foster parents also provides access

DOI: 10.4324/9781003231363-4

to financial and professional resources, and involves a duty of collaboration and confidentiality. Another consequence is that grandparents, aunts and uncles must adapt to the terminology of the CWS with regard to roles, relationships and practice. For example, having the description of one's role/status changed from grandmother to foster mother and from grandchild to foster child. Contact between children and their parents becomes known as legally regulated visitation. One aunt, the sister of the child's father, expressed it like this:

AUNT: The problem is that we are brother and sister, and that is completely different to the situation with strangers ... I have to say I find this slightly difficult, having a foster child from the family. Because we have to relate to each other as siblings as well, in addition to him being Morten's father. So it's not so easy, really ... I don't think it is.

INTERVIEWER: What is the difference?

AUNT: Well, take the decision that the child welfare services just came up with, that now he can only have him during the day, and if Morten's dad had been a complete stranger then the children's services would just have managed it – them, wouldn't they, and said that this is how it is and we wouldn't have had much say in the matter. But since he is my brother, it's completely different, isn't it.? Because he [her brother/the child's father] can come here any time he wants, you know ... Because we're family. And that makes it hard to draw the line, in a way, draw the lines for us ...

Contractual relationship and family life – the ambiguity of foster care

As we have seen, the relationship between the CWS and foster parents, including where the foster parents are related to the child, is regulated by the framework of the foster care contract. The contract is a civil, mutually terminable agreement. It regulates the responsibilities and obligations of the CWS and the rights and obligations of the foster parents. The extent of financial compensation and arrangements for follow-up are concretised in the agreement and in intervention planning. How the foster family fulfils its obligations in accordance with the contract is controlled through, for example, supervision. Contact between children and their parents is regulated by decisions of and formal agreements with the CWS.

Formal agreements presuppose the fulfilment of reciprocity, obligations and responsibility regardless of emotional circumstances. One takes on a task in exchange for defined reciprocal acts. The agreement is a time-limited, rational relationship between parties or legal personalities, as opposed to an emotional relationship between individuals (Engebretsen, 2007, pp. 109–110). The exchange in the foster care agreement consists of relatives, for example, grandparents, making a commitment to assume the daily care of their grandchild for and with support from the CWS. Implied in this are agreements about oversight by the CWS of the foster parents carrying out their "task" in accordance with the guidelines and framework of the contract. The reciprocity consists of financial compensation, and support measures as required. Another way of putting it would be to say that by entering into the contract the families move into the field of children's services, in the sense that the logic of the CWS will override that of the families. When contractual issues regulate established family relationships, and the relationship between these and the CWS, the following question arises: What does the foster care agreement mean, and how does this formal aspect affect family life and relationships?

Personal care and professional practice

Foster care in general, and kinship care in particular, can be described as hybrids. By that we mean the interweaving of the private and public sphere and the somewhat diffuse divisions between spheres and areas of responsibility (Egelund, Jakobsen, & Steen, 2010; Nordstoga & Støkken, 2009).[1] In kinship care there is a convergence of the contradictory logic and values of personal family relationships and those of official, professional practice. The contrast between providing care in the family, on the one hand, and in an official context, on the other, can be compared with that between the concepts of personal care, which refers to the emotional, informal, experience-based and the continuous, and professional care, which is linked to the formal, science-based and the fragmentary. In other words, kinship care, when regarded as an arena where the public and the private sphere intersect, involves conflicting rationalities. Put simply one could say that there is a dividing line between "caring for others" and "caring for each other" (Madsen, 2002, p. 11). The first refers to asymmetric relations and the latter to symmetric relations.

Table 4.1 presents features of the basis for action in personal and professional care. Personal care is anchored in the values and logic of

Table 4.1 Personal and professional care – different rationalities

	Personal care Family	Professional care Child Welfare Interventions
Relationship status	Private	Public/official
Basis of relationships	Affective/emotional	Rational
Duration of relationships	Long-term/life-long	Temporary/time limited
Reciprocity	Mutual assistance (unpaid)	Unilateral assistance (paid)
Basis of responsibility	Obligation, belonging, regulated by norms	Professional ethical guidelines, regulated by law
Power relations	Symmetric	Asymmetric
Agreements	Unwritten, informal	Written, formal
The position of children	The child in the family/ network	The child as an individual, a client
Social control	Informal	Formal
Rationale	Care-oriented	Goal-oriented

family life and close relationships. Professional care is based on specialist knowledge and the logic of the workplace.

So what is personal care? Personal care is built on interpersonal
relationships, developed over time and based on varying degrees of
mutuality. The relationships are informal and affective. They are often
long-term or life-long, and have a history and an expected future in
a network of other relationships. Care between individuals in a family network is personal. The principle of mutuality is the key to understanding how the pattern of support and assistance for each other
have developed over time. However, the access to assistance between
relatives can also be unpredictable. Help and support in any given
circumstance are weighed and assessed by the parties. That it is unpredictable does not therefore imply that access to help is completely
random. It is expected that support will flow both ways between the
parties and that nobody should end up solely as a provider or receiver.
In a family network it is also possible for someone other than the person receiving help to "repay" the help. For example, when a woman
is helping her sister, it is in reality their mother she is relieving, or to
whom she "owes" help (Holtan, 2002, p. 53).

Help and support among family members confirm family ties both internally in the network and to the outside world. Finch (2007) describes this as 'displaying families'. This implies display processes where individuals and groups demonstrate to each other and to a relevant audience that they are doing things for the family and thereby confirming the relationship as that of a family, defining to whom they belong and making the family contours visible.

The norms of family relationships based on kinship facilitate a mutual exchange of assistance and favours, but without the calculation of individual advantages. There is trust in the family that if assistance is required it will be available, and therefore an individual contribution does not necessarily demand immediate reciprocity. For many, a sense of duty or solidarity is a key characteristic of family ties, especially among the closest family members. Each individual has a sense of responsibility for the family community and feels an obligation to contribute. Solidarity is expressed by the willingness of each individual to renounce something for the good of another, and this shows that what on one occasion concerns one person also concerns the other (Østerberg, 1992). Family relationships based on kinship are special, particularly because of the sense of duty and responsibility towards others, which are often put into practice. Duty may also be more a question of morale than of individual sentiment. Morale is not based on formal rules, but implies normative guidelines for how each individual must act in certain circumstances. Care and support between family members are formed on the basis of norms of reciprocity, or that there is "a right time" in people's lives to either ask for or give assistance.

What, then, constitutes professional assistance and care? Professional assistance and care, in this context, are the realisation of the requirements and intentions of the Child Welfare Act. The relationship with the client is professional and formal, and in principle not person-dependent. The relationship with the client is fragmented; it is based on short meetings and is time-limited. The work is based on interventions and agreements, where areas of work and aims and objectives are defined. Specialists base their work on changeable professional guidelines and the knowledge, practice and models which are available and valid at any given time in the specialist field (cf. Chapter 2).

The more dominant role of the state in the care of children implies a widening of the authorities' area of influence in terms of standards of good parenting (Ericsson, 1996). This is to a greater or lesser extent true of parents in general in our society. For foster parents, the influence of the authorities is more direct and explicit because foster parents become part of the CWS. The concepts of informal and formal social control are useful in this context. Informal social control refers to the non-legal and non-formalised control that we are all part of as members of society, while formal social control is formalised and usually written down, for example, in legislation (Ugelvik, 2019). Making adjustments and "learning" how to be parents, which happens in daily social interaction, are examples of informal social control. Foster parents in addition receive formalised and obligatory training. Before being approved, foster parents are obliged to attend the course 'Parent Resources for Information, Development and Education' (PRIDE), which is run by the Office for Children, Youth and Family Affairs (Bufetat). Kinship foster parents are also obliged to attend courses adapted to their particular foster care category as early as possible. This is one of several examples of formal social control towards foster parents. Another example is that the CWS may make decisions the foster parents disagree with, for example, to do with visitation agreements with (birth) parents, how supervision is carried out and any conversations the CWS may want to have with the child.

Sharing benefits and burdens versus economic exchange

The characteristics and differences between care based on personal relationships, on the one hand, and professional care, on the other, can be described using theories from classical sociology. We are using the concepts *Gemeinschaft* (community) and *Gesellschaft* (society), developed by Tönnies (1887). The notions are ideal types which characterise collaboration based on different types of action and rationale. Community as *Gemeinschaft* is based on long-lasting, close emotional relations and traditional collectively oriented actions. Community – of which family is an example – in these relations is perceived as "natural". The ideal type *Gesellschaft*, on the other hand, is the term for community based on more fluid connections and strategic, individual-oriented utilitarian thinking (as in business life). The difference between these two types of community can be expressed as sharing versus exchange (Falk, 1999). In foster care, especially kinship care, there is a confrontation between these contrasting types of action and rationale. Many grandparents and aunts and uncles who are foster parents will, for example, find it difficult that contact with the children's parents is regulated on the basis of formalised plans and agreements. We could say that the ideals and goals of foster care placement (the "inner" life of families) are community and sharing, while the structural frameworks of foster care are characterised by economic exchange and utilitarian thinking. Clashes between different bases for action or types of logic in private and public sphere may create confusion and conflict about the values, understandings or logic which foster care should be based on. This might again result in a "scaling down" of the traditional practice of mutual help and support in the family network.

The financial remuneration given to foster parents is an example of the exchange/utilitarian thinking inherent in the structural frameworks of kinship and non-kinship care. This may be a sensitive topic for relatives entering into a foster care agreement. The mix of emotions and money touches on taboos in our culture, where the exchange between love and money is out of the question (Bourdieu, 1996). Economic compensation may change the way relationships are understood in a family context and give rise to questions of motive for the foster care agreement (see examples below). The family is the most typical institution in society where norms about un-selfishness limit the striving of its members for financial gain (Bourdieu, 2001, p. 167). Particular ways of doing things which imply inclusion, co-responsibility and generosity are expected in the family network, and there is an expectation that the family members have a "disposition" for unselfishness. Bourdieu describes this as mandatory feelings and a sense of obligation (Bourdieu, 1996, p. 22). This implies a combining of two outside expectations: first that family members must demonstrate their emotional belonging, for example, by taking care of the children of other family members, and second that the family members themselves shall feel an obligation to contribute to this (see also Chapter 5).

According to Bourdieu (2001) it is the symbolic forms of capital which count in the family. If we go along with this theory, the price (salary/profit) will have to be hidden or rewritten – or it remains uncertain what the price represents. The economy of symbolic forms of capital is an economy based on something vague and undetermined, and which rests on a "taboo of making things explicit" (Bourdieu, 2001, p. 213). Economic interests are suppressed or remain implicit, or one resorts to euphemisms, i.e. using indirect words or expressions when talking about economic interests. What is denied is the practice of exchange, as in the logic of economics. Unlike in economics, the symbolic constructions tend to conceal the act of exchange in the actual practice (Bourdieu, 2001, p. 184). Designating someone as a family member, for example, by saying that 'she is (like) a sister' is to exclude a self-interested logic which has utility maximisation as its objective.

It is not, however, only kinship foster parents who may experience discomfort at the thought of financial remuneration. This was also a general feature in the study of Ulvik (2003), where foster parents participated through qualitative interviews. Independent of where the foster parents placed their role on the continuum between parenthood and occupation, they perceived the topic of remuneration as illegitimate or sensitive. The discomfort was linked to the relationship with the child, the reactions of the outside world and the "negotiations" with the CWS (Ulvik, 2003, p. 178).

The foster family can also be seen as an arena where a "battle" about the prevailing logic is staged. Financial circumstances and economic gain can in this context have a symbolic meaning in the definition of relationships, roles and how to understand the family as an arena for growing up.

Zelizer (1994), in her analysis of the social meaning of money, points out that money as a form of payment has different meanings depending on the context, time, space and social relations. She claims that the understanding of money is affected throughout by cultural and social structures:

> Money is neither culturally neutral nor socially anonymous. It may well "corrupt" values and convert social ties into numbers, but values and social relations reciprocally transmute money by investing it with meaning and social patterns.
>
> (Zelizer, 1994, p. 11)

Our study showed how the understanding of money (i.e. remuneration) is adapted to the cultural values assigned to relationships. At T1, for example, the foster parents typically valued the absence of economic self-interest. In one highly conflicted situation between parents and foster parents, the CWS and the foster parents had collaborated to keep the remuneration hidden in order not to further increase the level of conflict. This is how one aunt expressed it:

> It was absolutely awful. (...) they [children's parents] said we only looked after the kids for the money. We just had to cut them out [the contact with her sister and the sister's husband].

Another put it like this:

> They kept lashing out at us. And the mother also thought that we were only doing it for the money.

Because of the cultural expectations that families should be there for each other, without any thoughts of financial gain, such criticism can really hit home.

Remuneration – between support and reward

The division of responsibility between CWS and foster parents and the financial remuneration of foster parents vary greatly from country to country. In Norway, there are also internal variations in the remuneration and wages received by foster parents (Official Report NOU 2018: 18). In addition there are differences in how both case workers and foster parents view questions of financial remuneration. Foster care remuneration is important, particularly for low-income families. As mentioned in Chapter 5, statistically, kinship foster parents are more often single and with a lower income level than non-kinship care families. For low-income families with fewer network resources and demanding care situations, financial support and assistance from the CWS may be particularly important – both for the welfare of the foster parents and for their capacity to care for the child. In cases where the foster parents wanted to focus on the private, personal relationship, money usually meant something other than wages and profit. Many grandparents, aunts and uncles we interviewed at T1 said that the money benefitted the child, for example, by enabling the child to take part in activities that would otherwise have been beyond the financial scope of the family.

We also found examples of kinship foster parents who felt that whole or partial economic responsibility for the child should rest with the authorities. The thinking was that the arrangement ought not to yield a profit, but neither should it involve a financial burden. The understanding of the role of foster parent in the intersection between paid work and private obligation is "negotiated" with the CWS, and views on remunerations vary. One uncle (married to the mother's sister) expressed his experience with two different case workers as follows:

> Well, with the first one you were left feeling that you were only doing it for the money. She [the case worker] withheld money, but he [the new case worker], he said: "It's something that you need and something you should have, simple as that." If everybody had been like him it would've been much more enjoyable to do this work.

The first case worker communicated an understanding that the aunt and uncle had a financial responsibility, while the second placed the financial responsibility with the authorities. This demonstrates how the case workers' differing interpretations of kinship care (as family or as intervention, cf. Table 4.1) can be played out. The uncle pointed out that it would have been more enjoyable to "work" if the rights to remuneration had been more clearly communicated by the CWS. For him it would have been better if the case worker had considered their caring for the child as work which the family was doing for the authorities. The money incentivised and rewarded the effort. The uncle understood caring for the child as something other than a private obligation and for him it was important to be valued as a "colleague". Our material from T1 showed that it was mainly when the foster parent role became too demanding that the family members defined their caring role more as something approaching work. This was particularly true where the network was weak on reciprocal obligations. Wages combined with increased involvement of the children's services might provide the basis for an alternative definition of the task. This would release the foster parents from some of the cultural expectations inherent in close kinship.

Children's understanding of financial remuneration

Financial remuneration for foster care was also an important topic in our interviews with the children during the period 2014–2015 (T3). At that time they were aged 19–29 and no longer children, but young adults. We will use examples from two of the interviews to illustrate how differently financial remuneration is understood. The first example is from the interview with "Nina" (aged 25), who had lived in foster care with her aunt since the age of 6. While Nina was growing up her aunt had cared for her and brought her up alone. Nina described her aunt as a "fantastic woman" who had "gone to great lengths" to give her a good childhood at the same time as bringing up her own younger daughter (Nina's first cousin) and working part-time at the hospital. According to Nina her aunt deserved every krone she had been paid by the CWS. Our interpretation of what Nina was saying is that she regarded the money as a legitimate support and an acknowledgement of her aunt's effort to give her a good childhood, not as a motive for becoming her foster mother.

A stark contrast to the above example is provided by "Henry" (aged 23), who also grew up with a single aunt.

> When I found out how much you get paid to be foster parents, I was a bit like, okay so having me is a job for you. And then it sort of became very obvious.

He was 16 when he discovered the extent of the remuneration – and that had been a painful experience:

> I felt a bit like: OK, right, so it's because of the money that I'm here.

Henry did not use financial remuneration simply to illustrate his aunt's motivation for becoming his foster mother, but also as an explanation as to why theirs had never been like a mother-son relationship.

The greater the problems, the greater the relevance of specialist knowledge

As previously mentioned, a large proportion of kinship care is characterised by the foster parents having a personal relationship with the child. The understanding of the child and the parents or the relationship with them does not necessarily change following a foster care agreement. This background can also influence the foster parents' view of what kind of knowledge is relevant.

The CWS provide access to their specialist resources through courses and advice. For many foster parents, training and participation in foster care-related courses can be an expression of a wish to learn from and enjoy the company of others in a similar situation. Others may perceive the search for fellowship with other foster parents as artificial, as illustrated by this maternal grandfather:

> I thought: Christ, what's the point of me going on this course? They're my kids in a way, aren't they?

When the interviews with the foster parents were carried out in 1999/2000 (T1), there were no specific courses for family and networks, and they therefore participated in courses with non-kinship foster parents. Some kinship foster parents told us that they felt ill at ease by how the children's parents and other relatives were described by non-kinship foster parents on the courses. One maternal grandfather put it like this:

> We heard many people talk about the big problems they had, maybe with foster children of a certain age. In the group work sessions when everyone is supposed to talk about the problems they have, we don't have any problems [to report].

The importance attached by kinship foster parents to specialist knowledge may also be linked to their experience of the child and the collaboration with the child's parents. In cases where the child had significant problems, the foster parents expressed the view that specialist knowledge was relevant. Where relationships between the child's parents and kinship foster parents were conflicted, some kinship foster parents adopted an almost professional caring role approaching that of carrying out a job. Their relationship with the child's parents might get relatively formal and fragmented. They often wanted a clearer status as colleagues of the child welfare professionals. In recent years, foster care training specifically aimed at kinship care has been arranged.

The responsibility of caring for even a child who is a close relative can at times be hard to cope with. At T1 in our study this was particularly true when everyday life deviated too far from the expectations at the time the agreement was entered into. The kinship foster parents sometimes lacked the range of knowledge required for managing the demanding situations which arose, for example, if the child had problems they couldn't deal with or they experienced difficulties linked to the parents. In such cases, contact with the CWS would be perceived as meaningful, as expressed by this paternal grandmother:

> And I even phoned her [the case worker] at home, completely beside myself – I didn't really know what to do. Not about the kids, but around the thing with the parents and that. So I called and asked: What should I do? Yes. I just rang and cried and talked and … well, to get advice and help and … So, using the child welfare services, well I have to say that has worked really well.

The challenges were many and varied, especially in cases of a lack of clarity in the areas of responsibility and structure of authority between the child's parents and foster parents. When the basis of the arrangement which was intended to be a caring act towards family members gradually became characterised by internal fighting and conflict in the family network, the situation could become very difficult. Such cases sometimes resulted in closer contact with the CWS, and the foster parents came to have a greater appreciation of the services' professional perspectives. Informal arrangements could be replaced by formal agreements, and the communication between parents and foster parents could be done through the case worker. This is in line with results from other studies (Farmer, 2009).

The child welfare services' access to private lives

In our interviews with kinship foster parents at T1 we discovered that it was common to regard talking to the children's services about private matters as disloyal (Holtan, 2002, pp. 120–121). This was illustrated by foster parents talking about the extent of their deliberations before turning to the CWS. One paternal grandmother talked about the first time she told them about the situation of her grandchild and how she opened up and experienced actually being listened to. She was later shocked at what she had done, but she felt it was the only way out. She said the way she was treated by the case worker was greatly significant for their future collaboration:

> And after that we have been constantly back and forth and contacted the children's services, all that sort of thing. You could say it's become quite natural really, over the years.

Opening up one's private life to the CWS can be understood as a process of negotiation. Contact between private and official parties which is characterised by dialogue can often form the basis of a more personal relationship between foster parents and case workers. This was reflected in the interviews, for example, by how foster parents talked about the case worker, the types of topic they felt were relevant to discuss with the case worker and the degree to which they referred to the case worker when giving reasons for their actions. This is how a married grandparent couple described their contact with the CWS:

> PATERNAL GRANDMOTHER: Well, we've had two visits a year, that's all. And of course that's just because they are obliged to make two visits a year no matter what, so it's not because we wanted it or that there have been any problems or anything like that. But they probably want to stay in touch too, just to see how things are. They [the children's services] always say that it's nice to come here, because here there aren't any problems of any kind, so …
> PATERNAL GRANDFATHER: Yes, well … It's a bit like an outing for them, they come out here from the town to have a cup of coffee and relax a bit, away from all the work and hassle.

Where the initial contact with the CWS has been characterised by mistrust it can be hard for foster parents to get into a mindset of requesting the specialist knowledge and services they offer. The combination of responsibility for a child being regarded as a personal responsibility, on the one hand, and lack of dialogue with children's services, on the other, can lead to family life being shut off from the CWS. The foster parents can feel controlled and monitored, and dealings with the services become more about playing to the gallery than a real collaboration. The position of power held by the CWS may be a threat to the authority foster parents need and that they themselves feel they have, towards the child and the child's parents. The next quote from a grandmother illustrates this:

> I got really angry with my husband once because he rang and asked if our daughter [child's mother] could spend the night here. I said to him "why on earth did you ring them and ask about that, we are the ones who know what's going on and who should make that decision, not them".

The grandmother did not want to relinquish her parental authority by asking the children's services for permission for her daughter to spend the night in the family's home without an arranged visit. It could also be that the grandmother did not trust the services to listen to them and did not think they would be able to arrive at a joint decision. This type of understanding could lead to foster parents failing to make use of the specialist help and services offered by the CWS. Processes like this can be understood with the help of Habermas's theory on the colonisation of the lifeworld (Habermas, 1987). Simply put, colonisation here implies the child welfare system's invasion (with their regulations, professional and financial rationality, etc.) of the private spheres of individuals or families. The grandmother's reaction in the example above can be understood as a defence against this colonisation of the lifeworld and the possible need to put up barriers.

One relevant question in this context is how child welfare workers experience working with kinship foster homes compared to non-kinship care homes. The article by Dimmen and Trædal (2013) which is based on interviews with case workers in the CWS helps us to find an answer. They show that case workers sometimes experience having only limited room for action in their encounters with kinship foster families. This was particularly true for the case workers who approached kinship care as family. For those who approached kinship care as intervention, however, the scope for action was greater – they gave the families less opportunity to sort things out themselves and greater opportunity for intervention. Intervention in the private sphere of the kinship foster families can, in other words, be challenging also for individual case workers. It should be noted that when the CWS assess whether a family is suitable as foster carers, the family's willingness to seek help is taken into account. That begs the question of whether the CWS look for foster families that are more inclined to treat the care as a professional occupation rather than as a personal, familial type of care.

Child welfare services as guardian and buffer

The relationship between the CWS and their clients can be described as an asymmetric power relationship in terms of structural power, knowledge power and symbolic power. The formal institutional power is consolidated by legislation which gives the children's services the authority to initiate interventions towards families. The position of power is also linked to the fact that the CWS control financial and specialist resources. The case worker–client relationship can also be described as asymmetric in that the CWS represent a form of expert knowledge and are the stewards of the prevailing ideas about the "best interests of the child".

In the daily life of individual foster families, the CWS have the decision-making authority in questions concerning the daily care of a child who is in their custody. The freedom to act is limited by the formalisation of agreements which would normally be agreed internally in the family. As we saw above, this may, for example, be about visits and spending time together during public holidays. Formalised agreement can, however, also shield relationships from difficult decisions which might have increased the burden on these families who often face a multitude of difficulties. In the case of internal disagreements, parents and foster parents may, for example, "negotiate" agreement via the CWS. How they manage questions of power between parents and foster parents is vital for the relationship between the parties. The CWS can distribute the power in families by regulating and specifying frameworks for visits and other issues where there is disagreement between the parties. This can lead to the gradual reduction or discontinuation of informal structures about duties and responsibility in the family network and replace them with formal agreement and more formalised collaboration.

Our study showed that some kinship foster parents, especially grandparents, had experienced the exercising of authority by the CWS as a misuse of power in connection with the foster parent approval process. For them, the services became a burden in a period when they needed support. This provided fertile ground for distrust which affected the future collaboration with the children's services. Many grandparents therefore wanted to avoid contact with them. Where the families themselves felt that they had sufficient resources – a clear authority structure and satisfactory co-operation between themselves, – the grandparents often found the exercising of authority by the CWS rigid and poorly adapted to their situation. One example of such exercise of authority could be families where extra supervision was established because the child's parents also periodically lived in the house. The involvement of the CWS, and their demands, for example, for regulated visitations and supervision, can be difficult to implement in the families. In cases where the case workers had a better dialogue with the families, it appeared that the parties were better able to understand the logic and decision-making of the CWS. This gave the families greater confidence that the services could be helpful and they were better able to seek advice and guidance when required. Grandparents, uncles and aunts could also use the CWS as a communication channel – a third party in conversations which could give rise to conflict.

Grandchildren with a foster child status

So far we have shone a light on the formal frameworks of foster care, the different opportunities and limitations these have for the families and how this is experienced. Grandparents, uncles, aunts and other family members are not the only ones who have to relate to such formal frameworks for foster care. In the case of an official care order and the placement of a child in foster care, the children are given a client status which they have not chosen for themselves. They are no longer simply grandchildren, nieces or nephews – they have also been given client status as foster children. For those who grow up in long-term foster care, like the children in our study, the authorities – the children's services, in the form of case workers, supervisors and other representatives – are present in their lives throughout most of their childhood. The last part of this chapter deals with how children in foster care portray the relationship between themselves and the CWS.

How the status of foster children is understood has changed over time. Previously, there was a stigma attached to the label "foster child" (Hagen, 2001). Today, the status of foster child does not determine a child's future in the same way as before. Today it carries associations of risk and possible difficulties as a result of an unwanted childhood situation – usually caused by the parents' problems or deviant lifestyle.

The position of foster children has also changed in recent years as a result of social work practice by the CWS aimed at strengthening children's participation and agency. User organisations have also contributed to strengthening the influence of children and young people in their encounters with the CWS and other official agencies. The relationship between the child welfare service and its clients (the children) is nevertheless unequal and asymmetric. The CWS are the ones with the authority to initiate interventions, the ones who control material and professional resources and the ones who are charged with managing the prevailing ideas of the "best interests of the child".

Children in foster care: agency in the encounter with the child welfare services

In one of our analyses we investigated the types of agency presented by young adults aged 18–22 (T2) when they talked about their childhood relationship with the children's services (Thørnblad & Holtan, 2011). We discovered great variations in how the children, as young adults, related to the services. One extreme was relationships characterised by collaboration and personal contact between children and the CWS. We interpreted this to mean that the ones who talked about their relationship with the services in that way regarded themselves as equal actors to those who worked in the CWS. We saw one example of this in our interview with Gunnar:

> So then I rang Kari [the case worker] and said: Come and get me, I've had enough. I can't stand any more of this. And then I stayed with her over the weekend ... five days maybe ... And then – so that they sort of started the process of getting me moved.
> I spoke to Kari and told her that I would like to go to a family around here – I didn't want to be 40 km away from my mates, but 13 km isn't so far. It takes 10 minutes by car. And then I said that I have always been an only child, but I would like to try to have foster siblings. And my current foster family, they have biological children and foster children. Like I said, one of my criteria was that I should be allowed to participate in the choice of the new family, and also that I wanted to be near my mates and to stay at the same school.

This type of agency is the opposite of the powerless actor who experienced the relationship with the children's services as marked by mistrust and conflict:

> You have to watch what you say to them [the children's services] and that ... Yes – because there may be consequences. They are not good at solving problems. They are very good at creating problems.
>
> (Girl, aged 18)

> They didn't want me in the children's services anymore. They – or the one who was my social worker, she didn't want me in the

children's services anymore. (...). But I did get some help from (the people she was staying with). But they tried to fight against the services too, in order to help me. And they even phoned somebody in the Government who had a lot to do with the children's services. And he said it himself that [the municipality's] child welfare office was the worst in the whole country.

(Girl, aged 22)

Between these two extremes were relationships which, in the way they were presented, bore a resemblance to that of sponsor and receiver, an actor position which we have called pragmatic actor. The asymmetry in these relationships is clear in terms of power and access to resources; however, there are negotiations between several parties about the appropriate approach to problems that arise. Just like "equal actors", these relationships were also based on confidence in the CWS, but the influence of the services on their upbringing and childhood was generally limited to welfare benefits such as financial support:

Yes, I'm still under the child welfare services because I'm a student, so ... it's tough having a job as well, and we get around 5000 [kroner]. Yes. It's just because of the money – if it hadn't been for the money I would have opted out a long time ago. As soon as I was 18. I don't really feel a need for the children's services.

(Girl, aged 19)

We also saw relationships characterised by distance and little direct contact. The control function of the children's services was accepted, but beyond that the relationship was presented as more or less immaterial for the (foster) children. We call this position compliant actor. Any collaboration or negotiations with the services about the situation, or need for support, were taken care of by the foster parents:

Well, there was the usual [follow-up] – where a supervisor turns up and – sees that everything's fine, and that sort of thing (...) I've never had any conflicts or problems or anything like that with the children's services.

(Boy, aged 18)

What can we learn from this study? Together, the four constructed types of agency give us an insight into the different experiences of the young adults, having had the CWS in their lives throughout the whole, or large parts, of their childhood and youth. For the "equal" and the "pragmatic" actor, the presence of the children's services was a re-source. For the "powerless" and the "compliant" actor, on the other hand, the contact had been a burden – either because they felt power-less or because the only reason they maintained contact with the CWS was a sense of duty. Among the young adults who participated in our study, many fall into the categories compliant or pragmatic actors. At first glance this may be given a somewhat negative interpretation – i.e. that children who grow up in kinship care ought to be taught how to acquire more competence in order to become "equal actors" in their encounters with the children's services. However, it can also be inter-preted as a sign that many children in kinship care grow up in families where they are more or less protected from the formal frameworks which are in place for their upbringing. This is in line with other results from our study where children and young people regarded their up-bringing as normal. We will describe this in more detail in Chapter 6.

Implicit in the realisation of children's right to be heard and to par-ticipation (cf. the Convention on the Rights of the Child) is the pre-sumption that "the best interests of the child" are reinforced through direct participation of children in decision-making processes. From that perspective the "equal" actor is an ideal. However, as we have shown it is not obvious that everyone regards it as useful or important to master or learn the "rules" for achieving a close collaborative rela-tionship with the CWS.

Who should make decisions about the best interests of the child when the child lives in kinship care? Should the CWS or the kinship foster homes (foster parents and children) assess whether the child would benefit from extensive contact with the services, or could this contact be taken care of by the foster parents? Questions like this show the need both for a debate around the professional aspect of CWS and for research on the shifting of the official boundaries towards the pri-vate sphere – what this means for those involved and whether this is a desirable development.

Conclusion

Our research has shown that kinship foster parents generally did not regard their role as foster parents as job-oriented. The personal re-lationship with the child was predominant. The vocational aspect emerged in times of serious conflict and difficulties in the relationship with the child, the parents, the network and the children's services. In other words, when the grandparents, uncles and aunts were burdened by their tasks, they understood their role more as an occupation/

profession. Another way of putting it would be to say that the logic changed from "caring for each other in the family" to "care work for the child".

As we have described in this chapter, the formal frameworks are a result of the institutionalisation of kinship care as an official child welfare intervention, and they reflect an expansion of the area of activity of the CWS. The widening of the child protection field also needs to be seen in a wider, welfare policy context where the relationship between official and private spheres is changing. Around the same time as the introduction of the legal provisions for foster care which prioritised kinship and networks Ellingsæter and Leira wrote the following:

> Families are finding themselves at the centre of processes of change where the boundaries between the official and the private are constantly changing and where new connections and norms for the relationships between the family, the labour market and the welfare state which wrestle with established values and practice are created.
>
> (Ellingsæter & Leira, 2004, p. 13)

Kinship care as a child welfare intervention is in our view an example of the shift in the boundaries between official and private spheres. There are several contributory factors to this shift. The emphasis in our society on diagnostication (Løchen, 1976), also known as therapeutic culture (Madsen, 2017), has resulted in an increase in specialisation within the majority of welfare institutions and also contributes strongly to the specialisation or professionalisation of foster care. Foster care is differentiated and specialised for different categories of children or according to the children's diagnosed needs. Special interest groups and user organisations also contribute to processes of professionalisation through demands for professional standards and conditions resembling those of the workplace. Another significant factor is the increased use by the CWS of commercial actors. The widening of the market for care services has given commercial interests considerably greater scope for defining the professional standards and financial frameworks of foster care. This has an impact on the foster care situation, including kinship care.

Note

1 The term "private sphere" refers to family and friends, the individual, hidden from public view, while "public sphere" refers to the political, visible, collective and accessible (Kielland, 2001).

References

Bourdieu, P. (1996). On the family as a realized category. *Theory, Culture & Society, 13*(3), 19–26. doi:10.1177/026327696013003002.

Bourdieu, P. (2001). *Af praktiske grunde: omkring teorien om menneskelig handlen.* (H. Hovmark, overs.). København, Denmark: Hans Reitzels Forlag.

Dimmen, S. A., & Trædal, F. (2013). Fosterhjemsplassering i slekt og nettverk - Handlingsrom og dilemmaer. *Tidsskriftet Norges Barnevern, 90*(3), 158–173.

Egelund, T., Jakobsen, T. B., & Steen, L. (2010). *"Det er jo min familie!" Beretninger fra børn og unge i slægtspleje.* (Rapport nr. 10:34). København, Denmark: SFI.

Ellingsæter, A. L., & Leira, A. (2004). *Velferdsstaten og familien: Utfordringer og dilemmaer.* Oslo, Norway: Gyldendal akademisk.

Engebretsen, E. (2007). *Hva sa klienten? Retorikken i barnevernets journaler.* Oslo, Norway: Cappelen akademisk.

Ericsson, K. (1996). *Barnevern som samfunnsspeil.* Oslo, Norway: Pax.

Falk, J. (1999). Ferdinand Tønnies. In H. Andersen & L. B. Kaspersen (Eds.), *Klassisk og moderne samfunnsteori* (pp. 59–70). Denmark: Bo Reitzels forlag.

Farmer, E. (2009). Making kinship care work. *Adoption & Fostering, 33*(3), 15–27. doi:10.1177/030857590903300303.

Finch, J. (2007). Displaying families. *Sociology, 41*(1), 65–81. doi:10.1177/0038038507072284.

Habermas, J. (1987). *The theory of communicative action, Vol. 2: A Critique of Functionalist Reason.* Cambridge, England: Polity Press.

Hagen, G. (2001). *Barnevernets historie: Om makt og avmakt i det 20. århundret.* Oslo, Norway: Akribe.

Holtan, A. (2002). *Barndom i fosterhjem i egen slekt* (Doctoral dissertation). University of Tromsø, Norway.

Kielland, E. (2001). En drøfting av begrepene privat, offentlig og privatisering. In *Kjønn og makt i offentlig omsorgsarbeid.* (Rapport. nr. 34, delrapport fra Makt- og demokratiutredningen 1998–2003). Oslo, Norway: Unipub.

Løchen, Y. (1976). *Idealer og relaiteter i et psykiatrisk sykehus. En sosiologisk fortolkning .* Oslo, Norway: Universitetsforlaget.

Madsen, C. (2002). *Spiller det noen rolle? - om hverdagen på nye og gamle sykehjem.* (Notat 4-2002). Bergen, Norway: Stein Rokkan senter for flerfaglige samfunnsstudier, UiB.

Madsen, O. J. (2017). *Den terapeutiske kultur.* Oslo, Norway: Universitetsforlaget.

Nordstoga, S., & Støkken, A. M. (2009). *Barnevernsinstitusjoner og markedsbyråkrati.* Oslo, Norway: Universitetsforlaget.

NOU 2018: 18. (2018). *Trygge rammer for fosterhjem.* Oslo, Norway: Barne- og likestillingsdepartementet.

Østerberg, D. (1992). *Sosiologiens nøkkelbegreper og deres opprinnelse.* 4. utg. Oslo, Norway: Cappelen.

Thørnblad, R., & Holtan, A. (2011). Kinship foster children: actors in their encounter with the child protection system. *Qualitative Social Work, 12*(3), 307–322. doi:10.1177/1473325011428187

Tönnies, F. (1979 [1887]). *Gemeinschaft und Gesellschaft.* Darmstadt, Tyskland: Wissenschaftliche Buchgesellschaft.

Ugelvik, T. (2019). *Sosial kontroll.* Oslo, Norway: Universitetsforlaget.

Ulvik, O. S. (2003). Penger, kjærlighet og arbeid: Et kulturpsykologisk perspektiv på fosterforeldreskap. In E. Backe-Hansen (Ed.), *Barn utenfor hjemmet. Flytting i barnevernets regi* (pp. 167–182). Oslo, Norway: Gyldendal.

Zelizer, V. A. (1994). *The social meaning of money: pin money, Paychecks, poor relief, and other currencies.* New York, NY: BasicBooks.

5 Who become kinship foster parents, and why? Gender, family roles and relationships

Kinship care in the age of individualisation

According to sociologists like Giddens (1991), Beck and Beck-Gernsheim (2002) and Bauman (2000), modern societies are characterised by increased *individualisation*. This implies that social structures such as gender and class become less important for how people live their lives. Individualisation is characterised by the needs, wishes and self-realisation of each individual taking centre stage. The Norwegian Child Welfare Act and CWS are examples of this individualisation, because they place the individual child and the rights of the child at the very centre (cf. Chapter 2). This is particularly noticeable in the field of foster care, where the attention is focused on the individual child who is moving into a "new family". The child's family is also considered, but the work is concentrated on the child and the child's situation.

Family and welfare sociologists have been known to disagree on how increased individualisation affects family life and relationships. Their views can be broadly divided into two categories. One claim is that we, as a society, raise generations where individuals put their own needs above those of others, and to a lesser degree feel obliged to help or care for family members when they need assistance and support. Here, care responsibility is understood as something one can choose not to accept, or can withdraw from, if it is at the expense of one's own needs. Others claim that despite increased individualisation we still experience a responsibility for being there for family and close relatives (Finch & Mason, 1993; Gautun, 2003; Herlofson & Daatland, 2016). Our study revealed both of these situations: examples of the opportunity to choose not to accept a care responsibility, and examples of obligations to take care of the child. We will discuss this further below.

DOI: 10.4324/9781003231363-5

Negotiations on responsibility

Finch (1989) and Finch and Mason (1993) have made an important contribution to the development of theory relating to support and help between family members. In their studies from the 1990s they developed theory on negotiating responsibilities based on analyses of assistance between relatives. Negotiation is an analytical notion referring to active actors, which theoretically comes under symbolic interactionism.[1] Negotiations about responsibility encompass processes of deciding how relationships can be understood, appropriate proximity or distance, and whether one ought to help and how (Almack, 2008; Finch, 1989; Hedin, 2015; Herlofson & Daatland, 2016; Holtan, 2002).

Negotiations between relatives or family members about responsibilities include both structural provisions, for example, gender and family positions, and the actions of the actors. By family positions we mean how closely related people are. Both Finch and Mason (1993) and our own studies (Holtan, 2002) have shown that social attachment to the family we grow up in and how we are related are significant in negotiations about responsibilities between relatives. Equally important to structure is the question of action, in that assistance between relatives is a topic of negotiation about when it should be given, by whom, for how long and in what way (Finch & Mason, 1993). Family structures and actions interact – kinship does not determine the relationships which develop (Rowlingson, Joseph, & Overton, 2017). A woman does not take for granted that her brother will look after her child long term just because he is her brother. He is her brother, and their relationship has a past, a present and a future which may be influenced by whether she asks him for help. This is how one aunt expressed why it was her, and not her siblings, who came to foster the child:

> It was quite natural, really, that it happened like this [that the aunt became the foster mother]. I suppose I'm the one who has always sort of managed the family ... Been the one who has sorted things out for everybody and ... you know, just got on with it when somebody needed help. My brother is ten years younger than me. Maybe that's why – I don't know. And my sister's been seriously ill and ... I suppose I was the first to settle down and have children, and to have proper family relations.

Responsibility and solidarity are core characteristics in kin relationships, especially between close family members. Solidarity is characterised by both parties experiencing a common concern, and by both being willing to sacrifice something for the sake of the other. Solidarity implies having empathy for how others experience the situation and being willing to do something to help the other person.

That someone takes on such a comprehensive care responsibility as "taking in" the child of a relative can also be understood in the light of the need to create and maintain one's personal reputation in the family network. Self-projection, the person you want to be seen as, may play an important part in decisions about taking on the role of carer for a child.

Since kinship implies networks, actions in one relationship between two people can also have repercussions for other relationships. In some of the examples we will discuss later in this chapter it will be apparent that the main reason for becoming a foster mother was primarily the consideration for other adult family members, while the consideration for the child typically took more of a back seat.

Two examples of the background to an agreement to foster

There are several reasons why children cannot live with their parents. Our material also shows a great deal of variation in the background to when and how relatives assumed daily care of the children, and when and how the CWS intervened. In other words, kinship care comes about not just for one, but for a variety of reasons. In order to provide an insight into the many backgrounds to how an agreement on kinship care arises, we have chosen two examples from our research.

Example 5.1   Unexpectedly and suddenly becoming foster parents

The first story was told by Linda, the mother of two children who were moved to a kinship foster home:

> I started taking drugs in the last two years before they moved away from me. Well, both the dad and I did, we started using a lot of drugs. And it just got worse and worse. We had no control over anything. I was terrified that my kids would be taken from me, and I put a lot of blame on the dad to the CWS, you know, to avoid being seen as the guilty party, sort of. Finally, everything just went crazy. That was ... the last few months, it was hell on earth to put it mildly. And Kamilla [daughter, aged 12] watched me being beaten up by Aksel [the children's father], and Aksel

went for Kamilla, because Kamilla tried to save me, and there were people coming and going in the flat at all hours of the night and day. Tina (aged 3) didn't go to nursery; she wasn't cared for ... And I could see myself that it just couldn't go on like this. And we weren't getting any sleep. I was so exhausted. And in the end, the drugs didn't even have any effect on me. My guilty conscience and my shame nearly killed me. I got to the point where I handed the children over to child welfare services.

Aksel's sister and her live-in partner had previously been friends with Linda and Aksel. In the past months they had observed Linda taking a lot of drugs. They tried to help, collected Tina at her nursery and for a while had her living with them. When the CWS were to place the children, they were keen to take Tina in, and were later approved as foster parents.

The older daughter, Kamilla, moved to Linda's sister and her husband and their two teenage children. For them, the move was both unexpected and sudden. Linda's sister and her husband had previously had little contact with Linda and her children and had little knowledge of the extent of the family's problems. They felt "forced" to help in the situation which had arisen. There was pressure from the maternal grandmother that Kamilla should "stay in the family". Linda's sister had recently started studying, something she had been looking forward to doing for a long time. Becoming a foster mother did not fit in well with her plans, but when she was asked, she felt it was impossible to say no.

The story of Linda, her children and the children's aunts and uncles illustrates the variation in the relationships between parents and children, on the one hand, and those who became foster parents, on the other. The couple who became foster parents to Tina, the younger child, had for a long time and in many different situations assumed responsibility for her, and had got close to her. They wanted to care for Tina, and also to help Linda and Aksel. There was a gradual transition from sporadically looking after Tina to becoming caregivers and finally foster parents.

Kamilla, the older child, on the other hand, moved to an uncle and aunt whom neither she nor her mother or father had a close relationship with. Her aunt and uncle were not particularly keen on becoming foster parents, it did not fit in with their life situation. However, they felt they were not free to choose not to accept the responsibility, particularly because of consideration for the child's maternal grandmother. This example shows how obligations can be negotiated within a network, and that several parties may play a part in the choices a family makes about becoming foster parents. The example also shows that kinship position *alone* is not sufficient to analyse the relationships between relatives. Established practice and history between, on the one hand, those needing help and on the other, those who give it must also be taken into consideration.

Example 5.2   A grandmother's battle

The other story we want to highlight here was told by Dagny, Johan's maternal grandmother:

> Well, the mum [Dagny's daughter] was on drugs and all that. And my other daughter and her live-in partner, they were really struggling, they couldn't have children. So they applied to take in Johan. But no way! So he secretly lived with me, and the nursery – well they were absolutely wonderful at that time. Talking about it now makes me want to cry. The two who were most involved with Johan, they told me that if there was ever to be an inspection or something was going to happen, they would take him home. You know, at the time I thought – well, I was really naïve, I absolutely thought that the child welfare services were there to help everybody. It was completely crazy, all the secrecy and stealth that was going on. And despite that, sort of managing to let him have a relatively normal childhood ... Well, he lived here for a time, until he started school, but then the headmaster learnt that Johan was living with me and reported it to the child welfare services. There was a court case, and the child welfare services put up a real fight to place Johan outside the family. But I think I must have had the best [lawyers] in the country. When Johan became mine, to put it like that, the woman from the child welfare services asked me "are you angry with me?". I said no, I feel sorry for you. And then I walked away (little laughter). Yes, a bit of a downturn for them, wasn't it, because the child welfare services always know best.

This story illustrates several of the circumstances we have previously described. First, the resistance of the CWS to kinship care (discussed in Chapters 2 and 3), and as a result of that the effort, and sometimes the real battle, experienced by many relatives in order to be able to care for the child. While the CWS promoted an understanding of the child as an individual, the understanding of the grandmother and those involved was that the child belonged to and was part of their family. The example also shows how close relatives looked for solutions in their own network, first by the daughter and her partner applying to care for the child, and then by the grandmother assuming responsibility.

Kinship care is usually the responsibility of women

In the above examples, women had vital caring roles. The stories were not randomly chosen. Kinship care in Norway and other countries, as it has been practised up to the present day, needs to be understood in relation to women's traditional caring obligations and responsibilities.

In four out of five families in our study, the foster mother was a relative of the child and had not married into the family (see Table 5.1). Similar findings were also seen in the international research literature on kinship care (Perry, Daly, & Macfarlan, 2014). Our study also showed that male relatives took on the responsibility along with a female relative or live-in partner. However, around one in every five foster mothers was a single caregiver. No foster arrangement was agreed with men who were living on their own at that time.

One mother whose child was living with her father and his live-in partner expressed it like this:

> It's usually dad's live-in partner and I who sort out most things. I think she was the main reason dad took him in. I suppose he thought that Berit was going to be the one assuming most of the responsibility for him [the son], sort of, so if she had said "no, I don't think so", he probably wouldn't have agreed to it, maybe, so I think she had a lot to do with it.

In the 60 families in our sample which concerned grandparents, there were 15 single grandmothers and no single grandfathers. These gender roles concur with findings from other studies of the grandparent generation in Norway. Herlofson (2015) found that grandfathers have less

Table 5.1 Relatives in foster homes according to gender, N = 124[2]

	Number	Percentage
Relatives, female	(74)	59,7
Relatives, female and male (grandparents)	(24)	19,4
Relatives, male	(26)	21,0
Total	(124)	100,0

contact with their adult children and grandchildren than grandmothers. The same grandmothers were also there both for their own parents and for their grandchildren. Like the findings from our study she found that grandfathers were more inclined to step in when grandma did it; when grandma provided help, the husband did too. This is a reflection of traditional gender roles and confirms what several studies have pointed out, namely that informal care for both children and older adults is first and foremost provided by mothers, daughters and sisters (Herlofson & Daatland, 2016; Holtan & Thørnblad, 2009). Despite the fact that men are more emotionally involved in childcare and family these days and that most women are working outside the home, the main responsibility for the well-being of the family community still falls on women (Aarseth, 2018, pp. 93–94).

The dominance of matrilineal kinship

Children in foster homes often come from single parent families where the mother has sole responsibility for the childcare. As many as 54 percent of the children in our study had lived with a mother who had sole responsibility for the child; 8 percent lived with the father and 23 percent lived with both parents (Holtan, 2002). In the survey for the project "The New Child Welfare Services" carried out in 2008–2009, the parent sample had a similar gender composition (Storhaug, Kojan og Kvaran, 2012). The report *Child Welfare Services in Norway 1990–2010* also showed that children of single mothers were over-represented (Backe-Hansen, Madsen, Kristofersen, & Hvinden, 2014).

Given that single mothers are over-represented among families subject to child welfare service intervention, we can reasonably assume that it is the family of the mother rather than that of the father who assumes responsibility for the care of the child. This is confirmed by our study. Close to three out of four children moved to the mother's side of the family. Children who had lived with both parents moved to both sides of the family. Where the child had lived with the father, responsibility was in the main assumed by his family.

More than half of foster homes on the mother's side were established with the maternal grandparents as a starting point. The child's paternal side showed a different pattern. Here it was not the paternal grandmother, but the sister of the father, that is to say the child's aunt who most frequently took on the responsibility for the child. That parents should help their adult children thus appears to be determined by gender, in the sense that the women step in to care for the children of their daughters, but not in the same degree for the children of their sons.

This can be defined as a *matrilinear kinship* arrangement where the care for the child first and foremost is the responsibility of the mother and then of the maternal grandmother. It seems that when the father is absent in his relationship with the child, his parents also become absent. The children's relationship to their father's family often depends on the relationship these relatives have to the children's mother. However, we also found several examples of the paternal grandmother having contact with the child and the foster parents, and from time to time providing the link to the child's father.

Grandparents as foster parents

So far, we have seen that women in various ways play an important role in kinship care. Another central aspect of who becomes foster parents is the position in the family of those involved. Kinship foster parents are generally family members who the child's parents grew up with, and not more distant relatives. In 48 percent of the foster homes, the foster parents were the child's grandparents, in 44 percent they were aunt and uncle and in 8 percent more distant relatives (see Table 5.2).

That grandparents are important caregivers for their grandchildren concurs with findings which show that assistance between parents and their adult children is common in our society (Gautun, 2003). The Norwegian Life Course, Ageing and Generation Study (NorLAG) mapped the expectations of the grandparent role.[3] In the Nordic countries, grandmothers rarely take on full-time child care in the way that is more common in the countries around the Mediterranean (Hagestad & Herlofson, 2009). According to the NorLAG-study, sporadic help between the generations was the most common type in Norway. More than 90 percent of grandmothers and grandfathers agreed that they should be there for the grandchildren in crisis situations, such as divorce and

Table 5.2 Relationship of the child to the foster parents

	Number	*Percentage*
Maternal grandparents	(49)	39,5
Paternal grandparents	(11)	8,9
Mother's sister	(23)	18,5
Mother's brother	(9)	7,3
Father's sister	(17)	13,7
Father's brother	(5)	4,0
Other relatives	(10)	8,1
Total	(124)	100,0

illness. Most of them looked after the grandchildren once a month, around one in three grandmothers did so on a weekly basis, while daily childcare only happened in exceptional circumstances (Herlofson & Daatland, 2016, p. 47). In general, grandparents felt that they were not responsible for bringing up the grandchildren. Instead they regarded their task as supporting the parents in their role and spending time with the children, doing things with them (Hagestad & Herlofson, 2009). A clear majority of the population felt that contributing to the economic stability of adult children and grandchildren first and foremost is the responsibility of the welfare state (Herlofson & Daatland, 2016, p. 46).

As shown above, the role of grandparents in today's society is distant from both that of educator and that of provider. Grandparents who become foster parents thus far exceed the usual expectations of grandparents in our society, where finding oneself having to deal with the needs of both ageing parents and grandchildren at the same time is described as a somewhat difficult situation. Data from NorLAG showed that 29 percent of grandparents with grandchildren under the age of 12 still had their parents alive (Herlofson & Daatland, 2016, p. 63). Some women have a considerable care responsibility. They come up against expectations of assistance and care both from their parents and from their own children and grandchildren. In the interviews with grandmothers in our study, several referred to the problem of not being able to do enough for the other grandchildren.

Grandma should help if she can

For some grandmothers, the role of being a mother is experienced as a life-long care responsibility. One grandmother said:

> I have always been there for my kids. And that's why … Well, it's obvious isn't it, if they need help or … I think it goes without saying, if you're fit and well then of course you should help.

Several of the maternal grandmothers had gradually assumed the daily care of the child long before the actual kinship care contract was agreed. These grandmothers gave plenty of examples of how they had been there for the grandchild and the child's parents. They had looked after the child at all hours, without clear agreements about timing, as told by this maternal grandmother:

> "Mum, can you pick up Sofie from nursery?" "Yes, when will you get back?", I asked. But she couldn't tell me.

The grandmothers had laundered the child's clothes and accompanied the child to birthday parties and arrangements at school and in the nursery. They told us about desperate situations where they received messages from others that the parents were drunk or drugged and had left small children without supervision, about situations where they had to search for the child far from the child's home, about children who said, "I want to stay with you, granny."

All the situations of everyday life where the grandmothers and the grandchild were together contributed to strengthening the relationship they had with each other. The grandmothers gave the children personal care, they were there for the child. This care was the starting point of them gradually assuming full responsibility for the child, of becoming foster parents. One grandmother told us about the turning point, when they made the decision that the child should live with them permanently:

> When the mum had the kid there was no peace for us. Sometimes in the evening and at night I took the car and drove to where she lived, just to keep an eye. It was a terrible time, just really awful. And when we saw all the back and forth between us and the mum, we agreed with her – we sat her down and told her that this can't go on, you're destroying the child, we can't continue like this. So then she was willing for us to take the kid.

The quote illustrates the grandparents' understanding of the boundaries of acceptable care and the suffering they had experienced by having a son or daughter with serious drug problems. The quote also shows how they used their authority to change who should assume responsibility for the child by confronting their daughter about the consequences of her drug use and way of life.

As previously mentioned, by taking on the role of parents, grandparents exceed the usual expectations of grandparents in today's society (Herlofson & Daatland, 2016). One maternal grandfather said this about the choice to take on the responsibility of caring for the child:

> These are not easy choices to make. One choice was for her to be placed with unknown foster parents. And the other difficult choice, even if it may sound a bit brutal, the other difficult choice was to choose that we would be her parents for the rest of her childhood.

And one maternal grandmother expressed it like this:

> Well, I have to say that I was having such a nice time, and ... It was just him [the maternal grandfather] and me, and I felt I could

really do things and ... I enjoyed travelling and ... with girlfriends and ... and, well, I really loved that freedom. I have to admit I wasn't keen to begin with, but obviously, my selfish needs weren't really that hard to push away, because I knew in my heart that if Anja was going to live with strangers, we knew that the status of grandparents doesn't count for much in those situations – so ..., I would have found that really awful, and really I wouldn't have been able to live with myself. But now, we have Anja here with us and we can see that things are going well, and the work is no trouble, worrying is much worse. So really, everything is good. I do complain a bit sometimes, when I'm finding it a bit hard, but on the whole I think it's going really well. But of course there's always ..., we're kind of never ..., there's always something, always something we have to do (...). But ... but we also gain a lot from it.

Here, both grandparents expressed a situation where the choice of becoming "the parents of a young child" was pitted against the fear of the child moving to an unknown foster family. The relationship with the child was a decisive factor in their choice. This can be seen as an example of "the compulsion of love", in that it illustrates the ambivalence in choosing a life situation with obligations and care responsibility which breaks with the general expectations of today's grandparenting role.

One's phase of life and family situation can be significant factors in the decision of whether to become foster parents. For those who are in a phase where young children easily fit in, the decision may be easier, as expressed in the following:

UNCLE: It was the heart, really [that governed the decision to become foster parents].

AUNT: We felt as if she was one of ours, you know, in that she – that we had had her since she was 18 months. I mean, she was just a baby. So we couldn't imagine her having to leave the family.

UNCLE: No, no, no.

Personal care – obligations and costs

As distinct from non-kinship carers, kinship foster parents are usually more personally involved with the children's parents and their situation. In our interviews with many grandparents, we heard about sons and daughters whose lives had been hanging in the balance because of drug use, and how they had tried to help them, tried to encourage them to change.

MATERNAL GRANDFATHER: you're left disappointed

MATERNAL GRANDMOTHER: Yes, you're left disappointed time and
again. So ... daring to be happy when things are going really well,
that hasn't always been easy. Because we've often thought that
now ... now they're OK, and now everything's fine, and then ... it
goes completely ... she hits rock bottom ...

MATERNAL GRANDFATHER: Phone call from outpatients: you need to
come and pick up your daughter, she tried to kill herself, and now
she's sitting here.

In a study of stress in the foster parent role, Vis and colleagues compared reported stress in kinship and non-kinship foster parents (Vis,
Lauritzen, Fossum, & Holtan, 2017). The foster parents completed a
standardised form with 120 statements, which they had to agree or
disagree with using a five-point scale. The questions related to their
understanding of both the child and themselves as adults and parents.[4]
Kinship foster parents reported less stress in relation to the child than
foster parents in non-kinship foster homes did. The authors explained
this result by the children in kinship care scoring lower in terms of
problems, as well as having adjusted better to the kinship foster home
than what might have been the case in a non-kinship foster home.

Kinship foster parents reported higher occurrence of stress in the
form of depression and difficulties with the partner compared with
non-kinship foster parents. Vis and colleagues argued that this outcome could be linked to kinship foster parents being personally
affected by the parents' problems in a way that non-kinship foster parents would not be. They also stated that in kinship foster placements
it is often the case that one of the parents is related to the child but
the other is not, something which may lead to difficulties between the
partners (see also Cuddeback, 2004; Farmer, 2009; Harnett, Dawe, &
Russell, 2014).

Care giving in kinship care implies a different kind of personal involvement to that of non-kinship care, and this has consequences for
personal and familial stresses and strengths. This is especially true
for the child's parents. Below is a statement which illustrates such
difficulties:

AUNT: Well, you could say – the reason we took the boy in was that
the dad didn't manage to have him, or couldn't cope, to put it like
that. That's how it started. And that's really when my husband
and I decided that if we were to look after him on a daily basis,
it would have to be done on a proper basis. So that my brother

wouldn't be able to say after a couple of weeks that he wanted him back, to avoid that. It had to be done properly like that for the sake of the kid. And that's when we contacted the child welfare services in order to get their advice, about how we were going to sort it out (...) The problem is really that we are siblings, and of course that is completely different from if it had been to ... strangers ... So I see that as a bit of a problem with having a foster child ... who is a member of the family, you know ... Because we also need to relate to each other as brother and sister, in addition to him being the father of the boy. So I don't think it's that easy, really. ... Take for example the decision just made by the child welfare services recently, that he will now only have him during the day. If the father had been a total stranger, the child welfare services would simply have laid down the rules and said that this is how it is and we wouldn't really have been involved at all. But since he is my brother, it's completely different, isn't it...? He can come to us any time, because we are family. So for us it's very hard to establish boundaries, you know, boundaries like that ...

In kinship care, public and private spheres are interwoven (cf. Chapter 4). When a home becomes a formal foster home, the freedom of action is regulated. Parents may, for example, feel ostracised from their own family by visiting arrangements which limit and regulate contact. Another example is grandparents feeling "squeezed" between the consideration for the grandchild and their own son or daughter. Becoming a foster home can thus "do" something to family relationships. In some cases, the conflicts between those involved can escalate to the point where the parents, the child or other relatives work to undo the foster home agreement.[5] See also Chapter 6, Fact Box 6.1 on different family types, which illustrates variations in collaboration and solidarity in kinship foster families.

Kinship care, a class phenomenon?

Research, predominantly from the USA, has shown that kinship foster homes are more often found in populations with lower income, education and labour market participation; and in that country kinship care can be characterised as a class phenomenon (Cuddeback, 2004). Research from Norway also indicates that educational level, labour market participation and income of kinship foster parents are somewhat lower compared with the national average of the female population of Norway and of non-kinship carers. At the same time, however,

Norway reflects a society that is characterised by public welfare systems, relatively small class differences and a high standard of living compared to the USA. Nevertheless, Norwegian kinship foster parents can be said to have some of the characteristics of the lower classes.

So far, we have turned the spotlight onto various aspects of kinship obligations and parenthood and shown how structural characteristics based on gender are meaningful for who becomes kinship foster parents. We will now discuss class-based features of the kinship foster parents' situation, with particular emphasis on the educational level, income and family status of the women. This is built on a study where we compared the situation of women in kinship foster homes with both the female population of Norway and women in non-kinship foster homes. For details see Holtan, 2002 and Holtan and Thørnblad, 2009. We have also used findings from the study Foster Homes for the Needs of Children (Backe-Hansen, Havik, & Grønningsæter, 2013). Our results showed that the educational level of women in kinship foster homes was lower compared with both the female population of Norway and women in non-kinship foster homes. Equally, Backe-Hansen, Havik and Grønningsæter found that kinship foster parents, both women and men, had a somewhat lower educational level than non-kinship foster parents, although the difference was not significant (2013, p. 37).

Women in kinship foster homes had lower labour force participation compared with the female population of Norway, but there was no difference in labour force participation between women in non-kinship and kinship foster homes. In the study of Backe-Hansen and colleagues, foster parents were asked about their participation in the workplace before they became foster parents. Women in kinship foster homes had been in full-time work more rarely and been a full-time home maker more often compared to women in non-kinship foster homes. The researchers suggest that the difference can be explained by the fact that the women in kinship care possibly had scaled down their work because of their age, or because the child was already living with them. After becoming kinship foster mothers, the proportion who stayed at home increased in both groups; however, the increase was smaller in kinship foster homes than in non-kinship foster homes. The difference in labour force participation between the groups after they had become foster parents thus became considerably smaller (Backe-Hansen et al., 2013).

The proportion of married or co-habiting foster parents was lower in kinship foster homes compared with non-kinship foster homes (Backe-Hansen et al., 2013; Holtan, 2002). However, in 2001, the proportion of single women in kinship foster homes was equivalent to the average in Norway generally.

The family income in kinship foster homes was also lower than the total income in non-kinship homes in our study. The same was found by Backe-Hansen and colleagues. The kinship foster families were over-represented in the lowest incomes, under-represented in the middle incomes and equally represented in the highest incomes (2013, p. 38).

Another aspect which should be mentioned is the impact of class on parenting practice. Stefansen and colleagues have shown how middle-class and working-class families have different understandings of children's development and needs (Stefansen & Aarseth, 2011; Stefansen & Farstad, 2010). For children in kinship care this could mean that they encounter a care and upbringing environment similar to the one they are already familiar with.

Conclusion

In this chapter we have turned the spotlight on grandparents, aunts and uncles, and the processes which lead to them taking on full-time responsibility for a closely related child. We have shown that it is mainly the women who carry this arrangement. Until the introduction in 2004 of new foster care regulations on the duty of the CWS to investigate fostering possibilities in the child's family and networks, the drive to foster came from the families themselves. Our material showed, for example, that only 19 percent of the foster parents were recruited by the CWS. From 2003, the CWS have in varying degrees, through, for example, the model Family group conferences and similar devices, taken the initiative to recruit foster homes in the child's family and networks. Whether kinship care *today* is characterised by the same gender roles and the same family roles which came to light in the kinship care in our study, we do not know.

In her research on adults caring for their own, older parents, Gautun (2003) concluded that it was too soon to see what impact individualisation will have on the inter-generational care obligation. She asserted that the consequences of individualisation will be more clearly visible when those born in the 1970s and 1980s become grandparents. Relevant questions for the subject of this book are whether future grandmothers will continue the parenting of their grandchildren as we have seen it so far, and whether the grandfathers will be more actively engaged.

Since the change in social policy in the 2000s which involved prioritising family and networks, the figures from Statistics Norway (SSB) show a moderate increase in the use of kinship care. A timely question is how the authorities will be able to develop kinship care as a child welfare intervention without contributing to traditionally gender-based care practice becoming hard-wired.

Notes

1 Symbolic interactionism emphasises that human beings actively create the social world around them. Among the important theorists in the development of this school of thought were Blumer (1969) and Schütz (1963). According to Schütz (1963) one has to start with the situational meaning, in concrete everyday use, in order to understand the social meaning. The study of language is a central starting point for studying social meaning.
2 The unit of analysis is foster homes. That means that more than 124 children live in these homes.
3 NorLAG is a longitudinal Norwegian study which among other things contains data on family and generations. The data were collected in 2002/2003, 2007/2008 and 2017. See also: https://blogg.hioa.no/norlag/om-studien/. The findings referred to in the chapter are all based on data from NorLAG and also summarised in Herlofson and Daatland's state of the art report, 2016.
4 The study used the form "Parenting Stress Index".
5 A survey from Vista found that around 30 percent of moves in family and network placements were unintended. The proportion in kinship care is not shown (Ekhaugen, Høgestøl, & Rasmussen, 2018 p. 19).

References

Aarseth, H. (2018). Familie og intimitet i endring – sosiologiske perspektiver. *Fokus på familien, 46*(2), 84–102. doi:10.18261/issn.0807-7487-2018-02-02.
Almack, K. (2008). Display work: Lesbian parent couples and their families of origin negotiating new kin relationships. *Sociology, 42*(6), 1183–1199.
Backe-Hansen, E., Havik, T., & Grønningsæter, A. B. (2013). *Fosterhjem for barns behov. Rapport fra et fireårig forskningsprogram.* (NOVA Rapport 16/2013). Oslo, Norway: NOVA.
Backe-Hansen, E., Madsen, C., Kristofersen, L. B., & Hvinden, B. (2014). *Barnevern i Norge 1990–2010. En longitudinell studie.* (NOVA Rapport 9/14). Oslo, Norway: NOVA.
Bauman, Z. (2000). *Liquid modernity.* Cambridge, England: Polity Press.
Beck, U., & Beck-Gernsheim, E. (2002). *Individualization: Institutionalized individualism and its social and political consequences.* London, England: Sage.
Blumer, H. (1969). *Symbolic interactionism: Perspective and method.* Englewood Cliffs, NJ: Prentice Hall.
Cuddeback, G. S. (2004). Kinship family foster care: A methodological and substantive synthesis of research. *Children and Youth Services Review, 26*(7), 623–639. doi:10.1016/j.childyouth.2004.01.014.

Ekhaugen, T., Høgestøl, A., & Rasmussen, I. (2018). *Kommunenes tilbud til sine fosterhjem. Et kunnskapsgrunnlag for Fosterhjemsutvalget.* (Rapport nr. 2018/10). Oslo, Norway: Vista Analyse.

Farmer, E. (2009). Making kinship care work. *Adoption & Fostering, 33*(3), 15–27. doi:10.1177/030857590903300303.

Finch, J. (1989). *Family obligations and social change.* Cambridge, England: Polity Press.

Finch, J., & Mason, J. (1993). *Negotiating family responsibilities.* London, England: Tavistock/Routledge.

Gautun, H. (2003). Økt individualisering og omsorgsrelasjoner i familien. Omsorgsmønstre mellom middelaldrende kvinner og menn og deres gamle foreldre. (Doktoravhandling). Universitetet i Oslo. (Fafo-rapport 420). Oslo, Norway: Fafo.

Giddens, A. (1991). *Modernity and self-identity: Self and society in the late modern age.* Cambridge, England: Polity Press.

Hagestad, G. O., & Herlofson, K. (2009). Småbarnsfamiliens støttespillere: dagens besteforeldre. *Samfunnsspeilet, 23*(1), 92–94.

Harnett, P. H., Dawe, S., & Russell, M. (2014). An investigation of the needs of grandparents who are raising grandchildren. *Child & Family Social Work, 19*(4), 411–420. doi:10.1111/cfs.12036.

Hedin, L. (2015). Good relations between foster parents and birth parents: A Swedish study of practices promoting successful cooperation in everyday life. *Child Care in Practice, 21*(2), 177–191. doi:10.1080/13575279.2015. 1005574.

Herlofson, K. (2015). Lengre liv, nye hjelpemønstre i familien? *Sosiologi i dag, 45*(3), 24–45.

Herlofson, K., & Daatland, S. O. (2016). *Forskning om familiegenerasjoner. En kunnskapsstatus.* (NOVA Rapport 2/2016). Oslo, Norway: NOVA.

Holtan, A. (2002). *Barndom i fosterhjem i egen slekt.* (Doktoravhandling). Universitetet i Tromsø.

Holtan, A., & Thørnblad, R. (2009). Kinship foster parenting; gender, class and labour-force participation. *European Journal of Social Work, 12*(4), 465–478. doi:10.1080/13691450902840655.

Perry, G., Daly, M., & Macfarlan, S. (2014). Maternal foster families provide more stable placements than paternal families. *Children and Youth Services Review, 46*, 155–159. doi:10.1016/j.childyouth.2014.08.016.

Rowlingson, K., Joseph, R., & Overton, L. (2017). The nature of 'the family' and family obligations in the twenty-first century. In K. Rowlington, R. Joseph & L. Overton (Ed.), *Inter-generational financial giving and inequality* (pp. 61–99). London, England: Palgrave Macmillan.

Schütz, A. (1963). Concept and theory formation in the social sciences. In M. Natanson (Ed.), *Philosophy of the social sciences* (pp. 231–249). New York, NY: Random House.

Stefansen, K., & Aarseth, H. (2011). Enriching intimacy: The role of the emotional in the 'resourcing' of middle-class children. *British Journal of Sociology of Education, 32*(3), 389–405. doi:10.1080/01425692.2011.559340.

Stefansen, K., & Farstad, G. R. (2010). Classed parental practices in a modern welfare state: Caring for the under threes in Norway. *Critical Social Policy, 30*(1), 120–141. doi:10.1177/0261018309350811.

Storhaug, A. S., Kojan, B. H., & Kvaran, I. (2012). Enslige mødre i kontakt med barnevernet. *Fontene forskning, 12*(2), 4–17.

Vis, S. A., Lauritzen, C., Fossum, S., & Holtan, A. (2017). Parenting stress among Norwegian kinship and non-kinship foster parents. *Nordic Social Work Research, 7*(3). doi:10.1080/2156857X.2017.1326977.

6 Kinship care in the light of family sociological perspectives

Family based on complementary gender roles

Over time, changes in the dynamic and structure of family life have been the subject of great consternation. When, as a result of the industrial revolution,[1] the extended family was gradually replaced by the nuclear family, the worry was mainly related to the loss of unity and the loss of family influence in everyday life. Someone who was less concerned about this development was the American sociologist Talcott Parsons (Parsons, 1955; Parsons & Bales, 1955). He claimed that the emergence of the nuclear family, consisting of a mother, a father and their children, was a result of the demand by industrialisation for mobility. Parson's arguments were built on a structural functionalistic perspective, where the various structures in society create stability and integration in society as a whole. To him, the nuclear family was the most functional family type in industrialised societies: a specialised institution whose main tasks were the primary socialisation of children and emotional support for the family members. In Parson's 1950s family, the roles were gender-divided and complementary – that is to say the father as the instrumental leader and provider, and the mother as the expressive leader and caregiver. In Norway, the nuclear family and the housewife ideal were important elements of post-war family ideology. As described in Chapter 2, the family understanding at that time also had an impact on the practice of the CWS, for example, as reflected in the increase in the number of adoptions in the 1950s and 1960s and in the development of foster care.

There was, however, resistance to Parson's functionalistic family model, especially from feminists in academia. The criticism, mainly developed in the 1970s, pointed to how functionalistic theories masked conflicts of power and interest in the family, for example, in relationships where women were economically dependent on men. There was

DOI: 10.4324/9781003231363-6

criticism that women's work in the home was not regarded as work and that violence and other family problems were covered up. Questions about *for whom* the family was functional were therefore asked. According to Parson's family mode, the exchange relationship between a married couple was mutually beneficial. The criticism posed questions about *who* benefitted most greatly from this arrangement. One result of this criticism was research which sought to uncover and display society's gender structures and the future conditions of women in the family.

Family as practice

Family research in the 1970s and 1980s was primarily carried out from the perspectives of women and gender. However, in the 1990s, a renewed interest in family sociology emerged. The academic revitalisation of family sociology can be understood as an answer to the social changes that had been taking place since the 1960s. There was a considerable increase in the number of women entering the labour market, divorce numbers were rising, many common-law marriages were registered, and later, lesbian and gay rights were recognised by law in many countries. As a result of these changes, "new" family types which challenged the nuclear family as a hegemonic family model emerged. Examples of such new family types were single-parent families, step families, co-habiting families, LAT-families (living apart together) (Levin, 2004) and same-sex families.

These "new" approaches in family sociology represented a shift from Parson's structural functionalism in several ways. Rather than representing the nuclear family as the norm, the diversity of family life was recognised and researchers began talking about famili*es* instead of *the* family. By moving away from the understanding of the family as a fixed unit defined by specific relationships, researchers also opened the door to other relationships being understood as family (for example, same-sex couples and friendships). As pointed out by Morgan (2011), the emphasis on fluidity in families is not only a reflection of concrete changes in family patterns. On the contrary, it also represents a shift in the perception of family in more general terms.

> In some senses the fluidity was always present for the simple reason that family relationships were never simply or uniquely confined within households, but extended out and across households in a relatively weakly bounded fashion. In some countries at least, there was always an element of choice as to who might, in this wider sense, "count" as family just as, in terms

of everyday experience, family relationships might overlap with friendships and neighbourhoods.

(Morgan, 2011, p. 21)

The last change we would like to highlight here, and which is closely linked to the previous point, is the shift towards a more dynamic understanding of family. The British family sociologist, David Morgan, has been particularly influential in this regard. According to Morgan (1996, 1999), family can no longer be understood as a structure or institution to which people belong, but rather it should be approached as a set of practices. Only through the way families practise their family life can we look more closely at what it is that constitutes what people experience as their family.

We must therefore, according to Morgen, accentuate the idea of *doing* family. From this perspective, family is thus not a given, but rather something that is created through action. Someone who has further developed this perspective is Janet Finch (see also Chapter 4). According to Finch (2007), family practices are not sufficient in themselves – they also have to be *displayed*:

> (...) the meaning of one's actions has to be both conveyed to and understood by relevant others if those actions are to be effective as constituting 'family' practices.

(Finch, 2007, p. 66)

One example from our interviews which illustrates both these aspects of family life – both practice and display – is the interview with Karsten:

> I've always been a part of the family, you know. For example, mum has been in and out of hospital a few times because of illness, and it was often me going with her because dad didn't always have time. And every time they asked her who was accompanying her, she always said, "it's my son". So, not foster son or anything like that.

(Karsten, aged 26)

Stability and change

One important question which arose in line with the professional re-orientation was, and continues to be, how different today's families *really* are: how radically different is today's family life compared to earlier? According to sociologists like Beck and Beck-Gernsheim (1995, 2002), today's families reflect a specific time where traditional guidelines and limitations have been replaced by, for example, reflexivity, autonomy and unpredictability. Action and choice are based on interpretation and critical assessment rather than on custom and tradition. This argument belongs to the thesis of individualisation, which we also referred to in Chapters 2 and 5. From a perspective of individualisation, family, however it is constructed and centred, becomes something new where traditional rules are replaced by the individual and their needs.

The individualisation and de-traditionalisation thesis has been widely supported in family sociology; however, it has also been challenged by many. Gilding (2010), for example, argued that in the same way as sociologists previously over-emphasised convention, they are today over-emphasising reflexivity. Gilding claims that reflexivity and freedom of choice do not necessarily involve actions that break with traditional guidelines for how one should or must live. Using examples, including from practices linked to questions of inheritance, he demonstrates that traditional family conventions are also important today. To transform, or as he puts it to reconceptualise, family as *reflective practices* would be to throw the baby out with the bathwater. Kinship care is an example which supports Gilding's point, because as we saw in Chapter 5, taking over the daily care of a closely related child can be a question which, for many, is not experienced as a choice unless one has good reasons for saying no. Traditional aspects of family practice are also seen, in that it is primarily female relatives who assume the responsibility of care. These are examples of how traditional family conventions are expressed in our society today.

Changing patterns of parenthood

We will now focus on parenthood and the characteristics of parenthood today as described in sociological research. Our discussion will concentrate on two trends, the first is the central position of children in today's families and the second the increased importance attached to the father.

As described above, the individualisation thesis is also present in the descriptions of today's parenthood. An important concept in this connection is Giddens's notion of the "pure relationship" in postmodern society (Giddens, 1992). In a *pure relationship*, which in Giddens's view is characteristic of personal relationships, the duration of relationships is uncertain. The mutual satisfaction of the parties and the assessment of the quality of the relationship is a continuous process. Maintaining the relationship requires the mutual trust and continuous choice of staying together, as well as the wish to *uphold the relationship for its own sake*. According to Beck and Beck-Gernsheim (1995), shifts in personal relationships and individualisation also contribute to changes in the meaning of parenthood. At a time when the personal relationship of a couple no longer is a guarantee for security and continuity in and between adults, the child becomes a kind of provider of ontological security for individual parents.

Like other family research, sociological theories of parenthood reflect a shift away from the static to the active and fluid. The shift is illustrated by the distinction between the concepts of *parenthood* and *parenting*. Whilst parenthood refers to social norms for and expectations of parents, parenting is the execution of parenthood through various practices. Like Beck and Beck-Gernsheim, a number of family researchers have pointed out that our current understandings of parenthood and the practice of parenting are more child-oriented than before. The availability of parents, like the housewives of former years, is no longer sufficient and does not fulfil today's understandings of what children need. The norm is for parents to be involved and to participate in the lives of children. Forsberg (2010) has called the current child-oriented parenting *involved parenting*. This implies that parents are not only responsible for their children, but they are also expected to spend time with them in order to develop a close relationship.

Hays (1996) preceded Forsberg with her conceptualisation of a similar development of mothering with the term *intensive mothering*. This type of mothering is "expert guided" and "child-centred". The child's mother in particular is seen as fundamentally responsible for all aspects of the child's development, whether physical, emotional, social or cognitive. In everyday family life the needs of the child are of prime importance and those of the parents, especially the mother, come second. The drivers of this demanding model of parenthood are professions, market forces and social norms.

Descriptions or characteristics such as *involved parenting* and *intensive mothering* point towards ideals, trends and processes of change in our society today. However, as emphasised by Stefansen (2011, p. 23), it is not obvious which actual *responsibilities or practices* are involved in such ideals. In other words, the predominant discourses on parenthood and parenting in any given period are something that all members of society relate to; however, they affect people in different social classes in different ways.

In Forsberg's study of Swedish middle-class families with children, *involved parenting* implied that the parents prioritised making time in order to create a close relationship between themselves and the child.

He refers to Halldén's (1992) ideal types – *the child as a being* and *the child as a project*. The child as a being refers to understandings of children and young people as a natural process driven by inner forces. The task of the parents is to be there for the child, but the child's development may, but should not, be unnecessarily influenced. On the other hand, parents of "children as projects" are very important for the children's development, and, according to Forsberg, also important for the middle-class parents' own identity.

The changed demands of parenthood are expressed in different ways in today's society in general and in the CWS in particular. Examples of this are systematic training and guidance for foster parents, and the fact that an increasing number of foster parents are freed from having to work outside the home. Training and follow-up of foster parents, as well as the facilitation of arrangements which otherwise are not available to parents, can be interpreted as increased attention on the needs and security of children. But it also reflects an understanding that children who are in the care of the authorities are a group with different needs from other children. It is therefore no longer sufficient for foster parents to simply "take in" children – they also have to be developed as skilled caregivers for children with particular needs.

The father as parent

The current understanding of parenthood and parenting must be viewed in relation to the changing understandings of the needs of children and young people. Development psychology has played an important part in this regard. One example of the contribution of development psychology is the knowledge of the importance of the interaction between caregivers and the youngest children, that it is interpersonal contact and interaction which stimulate infant development (Stern, 1985). As pointed out by Haavind, this knowledge was primarily communicated to mothers:

> Psychology presented the social and communicative potential of the small child as a message to the mothers (...). The same professionals were not in a rush to tell fathers what they would miss if they didn't begin to interact early.
>
> (Haavind, 2006, p. 686).

Even though mothers and fathers still receive different information about how they should be involved in their children's lives, there is little doubt that understandings and practice of the father's role have changed considerably over the past decades. As seen above, the father's role in Parson's functionalistic family model was limited to providing for the family and exercising authority. Today's fathers not only spend more time with their children than before (Kitterød & Rønsen, 2013), but they must also, as Haavind points out, be held to account if they do not participate in the care of children (2006, p. 683).

Brandth and Kvande's (2003) concepts *absent fathers* and *flexible fathers* describe the changes and challenges linked to traditional ideals of fatherhood. The concept *absent father* refers to traditional types of practice where masculinity and fathering are to a great extent linked to power/authority and the responsibility to provide for the family. The term *flexible father* refers to the changing nature of masculinity in the sense that men participate in arenas previously reserved for women. Between the "traditional and absent father" and the more "present and flexible modern father" we find variations in how fatherhood is shaped, and the research describes the characteristics of *different* fathers' roles (Brandth & Kvande, 2003). According to Plantin (2001), research into modern fatherhood presents a fragmented and contradictory picture. On the one hand, a large number of studies show that a traditional gender division in family and childcare is still largely maintained (Smeby, 2017). On the other hand, today's fathers differ from previous generations, in that they are more engaged in their children's lives and are generally more family-oriented. With this in mind, Plantin proposes that instead of using terms like "traditional" and "modern", fatherhood today should be viewed as different positions on a continuum between traditional expressions and a more democratic participation in family life.

Kinship care – how family is understood by children, teenagers and young adults

In the previous paragraphs we have described theoretical perspectives linked to family and parenthood/parenting. We have seen that current family types, family practices, family relationships and family establishment are characterised by variation. This distinctive feature of family life which Syltevik (2000) describes as *differentiation* is also expressed by families who are included in the kinship care category.

There are many reasons why children are moved out of their parental home and into foster care with relatives. The most common grounds are the parents' substance abuse and neglect, but it can also be parents' mental illness or death and other circumstances. Many

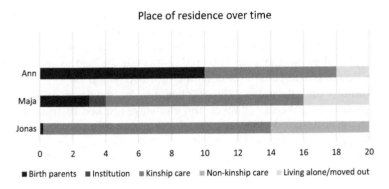

Figure 6.1 Examples of place residence over a period of time.

children are moved at a very young age,[2] and remain with relatives for varying periods, some for a relatively short while and others throughout their whole childhood.

Figure 6.1 illustrates places of residence over a period of time for three of the informants in our study (Skoglund, Thørnblad, & Holtan, 2018).

As we saw in Chapter 5, many moved to grandparents, others to uncles and aunts and some to other relatives. The degree of involvement of the CWS varied; some experienced the children's services as closely involved during their childhoods, while for others they were perceived as almost invisible or somewhere in the background (Thørnblad & Holtan, 2011). There was also variation in the children's relationship with their parents, in the relationship between the foster parents and the children's parents and in the parties' understanding of what kinship care was meant to be and should involve. As shown in Chapter 5, it is important that the act of assuming the care of a child is understood as a topic of negotiation about when the care shall be given, by whom and in what way. This is important for how kinship care is organised and practised. Based on the analysis of obligations and relationships, some kinship foster families resemble divorced families where the children have relationships with two families, while others have a closer resemblance to nuclear families. Others again are closer to traditional, extended families with three generations including both the child and the child's mother. Fact Box 6.1 shows one of several ways to illustrate variations in family life.

FACT BOX 6.1   Family types in kinship care (Holtan, 2002, 2008)

The family types were developed from qualitative interviews with children growing up in kinship care and their foster parents and parents. The family types do not exist in pure form, but are constructed based on the following criteria: *understanding of the foster care assignment, power* and *solidarity*.

The extended family: The foster care assignment is understood as a joint family project where the foster parents' understanding of family is open and inclusive towards the parents. The children include both parents and foster parents in their understanding of family.

The multi-nuclear family: The foster care assignment is understood differently by the foster parents and the parents with both parties considering themselves to be the centre of the children's lives. The child describes the family as two family sets: the birth family and the foster family.

The monopolising family: The foster care assignment is understood differently by the foster parents and the parents, with both parties considering themselves to be the centre of the children's lives. It is different from the multi-nuclear family in that these relationships are characterised by low solidarity and a lack of trust, something which often leads to conflict. The parents may, for example, want greater participation in the children's lives, but the foster parents want to limit it.

The broken family: A result of prolonged processes of conflict between the parents and the foster parents, which over time leads to a break in the relationship between the foster parents and parents. The child has in reality no contact with their parents.

Biological family: The children have a strong, biologically anchored family understanding by exclusively including their biological family in the definition of family. The children have very little space for a close relationship between themselves and the foster parents. A common feature of this family type is that the children are often older when they are moved from the parents.

Family understanding and normality

One general feature in studies on kinship care where children, teenagers and young adults have been interviewed is that many characterise their family and their upbringing as normal. This is also reflected in studies carried out in countries like Denmark (Egelund, Jakobsen & Steen, 2010) and Scotland (Burgess et al., 2010), as well as in our own studies in Norway. It is important to ask what normality means in this context, but another important question is also: how are we meant to understand that some children, teenagers and young adults describe their upbringing and family as abnormal?

According to Grue (2016), the concept of *normal* entered European languages in connection with the development of statistics and science in the 19th century. By using modern statistical techniques, scientists were able to define the mean, normal distribution and deviation. In other words, normality is not something which exists independently of us humans, it was created through instrumental measurements, for example, of weight and height. Normality is not only limited by normal distribution curves and standard deviation, but also by the legitimisation of certain ways of living which are perceived to be right and good at a given time in a given society (Solvang, 2006, p. 168). Today, the term normality is widely used in everyday speech, and we often have an intuitive idea of what is meant when something is said to be normal or abnormal. The term is also context-dependent, and what is "normal" can be understood differently by different people at different times. Normality is therefore a relative concept with undefined limits (Grue, 2016, p. 12).

In the kinship care study by Egelund, Jakobsen and Steen which was based on qualitative interviews with Danish teenagers and young people aged 13–20, normality related to the fact that their upbringing was not one "which requires too many explanations" (2010, p. 12). We recognise this understanding from our own study. In our studies as well as those of others with similar results, this feeling of normality is emphasised as something positive. We will discuss the reason for this in more detail.

In order to understand why normality is considered to be a good thing in this context we need to go back to one of the issues we discussed in Chapter 4. Here we showed that kinship care can be understood as an arena where there is an intersection between the private and the public, and how the different rationales of the two spheres can come into conflict. One of the examples we used was financial remuneration. Remuneration can be a sensitive topic precisely because it goes against what is understood as normal when it comes to taking care of children. For children, the knowledge that their foster parents get paid can make them question their relatives' motives for caring for them.

Another example of intersecting rationalities which we also mentioned in Chapter 4 is that terms which confirm relationships, roles and practice are replaced by the specialist terminology of the CWS – families become *foster homes*; grandparents, uncles and aunts become *foster parents*; grandchildren, nieces and nephews become *foster children*. The terms *foster child* and *foster family* have a distinguishing function and give children a client status which they have not chosen for themselves; rather, it is a formal attribution which accompanies the foster care agreement. The term is associated with burdens caused by a childhood situation, usually caused by the parents' problems or deviant lifestyle. This means that when children who grow up in foster care talk about themselves and their upbringing, various understandings of risk and vulnerability may emerge. These are notions linked to the current status of foster children. However, the foster child status also provides opportunities which are not available to other children. An example of this is that children growing up in foster care are followed up according to the law by supervisors in order to ensure that their needs are met and that they are not suffering neglect a second time. In such meetings, which are held without the presence of the foster parents, the supervisor wants to hear how the children are, whether they are happy, what their needs are, and so on.[3] This enables the children to evaluate their foster family and to suggest any necessary changes. The children can submit complaints, and negotiate new everyday routines (for example about bedtime and screen time) via an "external body". Children and young people who do not grow up in care do not have the opportunity to do this. They can of course always tell their parents that they want to go to bed later, but in the end it is the parents who decide. The point we want to make here is that the formal framework can influence how the foster family works and is understood, and also how children and young people understand themselves and their place in the family. In other words, the frameworks which are put in place to prevent children from experiencing neglect can also have unintentional, negative consequences. Frameworks with the intention of providing normality for children by giving them the right conditions to grow up in also involve giving children a foster child status, which may lead them to view themselves as clients.

In the interviews with children, teenagers and young adults in our study about growing up in kinship care we discovered that the logic of child welfare authorities hardly came up in their stories or not at all. However, even when someone's childhood and family relationships are described as ordinary or normal, the formal framework represents something which is not ordinary when compared with children and young people who do not grow up in the care of the authorities. For some, the presence of children's services during their childhood can therefore be experienced as a breakdown of their understanding of the meaning of normality. The normal, the unusual and the alienating are particularly well reflected in our interview with "Joakim" (aged 21 in 2015) in one of our studies (T3):

> In a way it's just an ordinary childhood with – with a bit of a twist – with a little more … irritation, in a way, or whatever you want to call it – a little more disturbance from the child welfare services. Who come in to ask if we're okay – when we are, you know? And we – or rather I – was absolutely fine. I've always had a very good childhood. So, there haven't been any … there haven't been any big problems. The story of my childhood is not really very exciting, even if it was in foster care.

Even if normality was emphasised by many of the informants, it is important to stress that this was not the case in all the interviews we carried out with children, teenagers and young adults who had grown up in kinship care. We also came across those who understood family as foster care and themselves as foster children. There are also in-between positions where aspects of both foster care and ordinary family life are present. Figure 6.2 illustrates how the different understandings may be weakly or strongly associated. The blue circle represents foster care and the orange circle represents family. The circles have their own built-in logics from professional activity and the family sphere, respectively (cf. Chapter 4). The circles with the greatest distance from each other illustrate how kinship care is understood by children and young people when the logic of the CWS is practically absent in family life. The other extreme, where the circles are close to each other, illustrates how kinship care is understood when it is more or less understood as a CWS intervention.

Absent fathers?

Many of our informants presented normality as a feature of their upbringing, but this is not the same as saying they had a problem-free

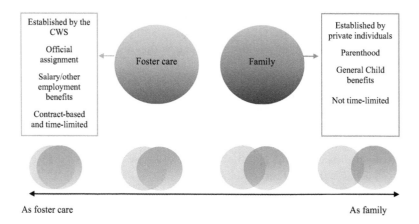

Figure 6.2 Understandings of kinship care.

childhood. What any such challenges may involve, how they are interpreted and the space they occupy in the lives of children, teenagers and young adults vary and may change over time. There are, however, some challenges that repeatedly crop up in our studies, and they relate to the children's parents.

As shown in the previous chapter, kinship care was characterised by children generally moving in with their maternal grandparents or aunts. This gender-divided picture was reinforced by most children having only limited or no contact with their fathers. That was true both before the children moved out of the parental home and in connection with visitation while the children were in kinship care. This gender-division pattern is also seen in child welfare statistics generally (Storhaug, Kojan & Kvaran, 2012). As shown in a study by Storhaug (2015), the attention of the CWS was in the main directed towards mothers, since they were often regarded as responsible for the family and the well-being of the children. In order for the CWS to define fathers as part of the child's family, a certain participation was required on the part of the fathers. According to Storhaug, a biological relationship did not suffice. In our study, one of the mothers said this about society's different expectations of her and the child's father:

When we attended BUP [the Child and Adolescent Psychiatric Out-Patient Clinic], nobody ever asked about the father. The only thing they asked about was his name.

The terms *flexible* or *present* fathers we referred to above, therefore, have only limited relevance when describing how the children's fathers exercised their parenting roles. As always it is important to stress that there is variation, that children who grow up in care can also have fathers who are present, and engaged in their lives.

That said, absent – though in different ways – fathers are a main feature of our informants' representation of their fathers and their relationships with them. They can be fathers who have never been in their lives, or with whom they have had unstable, infrequent or unpredictable contact. For most, the absence of their fathers was a factor throughout their whole childhood. That was also the case for Erlend (aged 20), whom we interviewed (T2).

> I've met him, but I've not had any regular contact with him. Just from time to time, every now and then … Like, every 4–5 years.

For some the relationship with their father changed somewhat over time. This appears to often be dependent on the father's substance abuse or other problems:

> Well, he was drinking heavily until I was about 13–14. He kept contacting me when he was drunk. I never heard from him when he was sober. When I was around 14 I think, he went into rehab, so I had had a bit of contact with him then.
>
> (Girl, aged 20)

Inadequate mothers?

Another feature of the data in our three doctoral theses is that mothers were included in the stories told by our informants, and that the mothers were part of their family network. Most of them had had relatively continual contact with their mothers throughout their upbringing, but the extent and form of the contact varied:

> Well, I talk to her on the phone, and then I go and see her from time to time on a weekend, to relax – get out into the countryside.
>
> (Boy, aged 18)

The mothers of children who grow up in long-term foster care do not live up to the current understanding of parenting. Not only do they break with the ideals of involved parenting in terms of presence and follow-up in the children's lives, but they have also been assessed by the CWS as unsuitable parents for their children. One of the women interviewed at T1 described the last meeting with her daughter like this:

MOTHER: I have always felt that I have been unable to fulfil her needs when she comes to see me. She expects something very special to happen, I almost think she expects that everything is going to be okay. Even if I'm sure she knows that nothing special is going to happen. But she still hopes that I'm going to say that she can move in with me. But she seems to wait for something wonderful which is going to change everything.
INTERVIEWER: Does she express this openly?
MOTHER: No, she doesn't. It may just be a feeling I have. But... I feel that neither of us have achieved exactly what we wanted in a way, when she leaves.

Parent-child relationships practised when children are growing up in foster care or kinship care do not only challenge norms about how this should be done, but also our linguistic repertoire. Mainstream linguistic codes in our culture are not always suitable for the situations or intersection of actual roles and relationships which are found in individual foster families. Thus, when children, teenagers or young adults need to find ways of expressing their family situation in kinship care it can sometimes be a bit of a challenge:

My mum's more like my best friend than a mum, in a way. Because we have a lot of things in common. I've discovered over the years that we are very similar, and ... she recognised many of the problems I've had, teenage problems and that. So my mum's been my best friend, really.

(Girl, aged 20)

She [the mother] is not the one who has been telling me to go to bed and brush my teeth and ... taking me to school, and things like that. So, you know, I argue with my grandmother the way normal people argue with their parents. People say to me "I don't understand how you dare talk to your granny like that". But then I say, well "yes, but my granny is sort of my mum".

(Girl, aged 25)

By redefining the relationship – from mum to girlfriend – it is sometimes easier for children to relate to mothers who do not live up to the ideals of motherhood. When they grow up, children who assume the role of carer towards their parents also sometimes use a different language to describe the roles, reflected in the following example:

> It's a terrible thing to say, but I do feel that I don't love her in that way, because she has never behaved like a mum towards me. Instead she has kind of been like a little sister, someone I have to tell what to do and what she can't do. "That was stupid", sort of thing. So ... No, she has never been like a "mum". She's been a drug addict since she was 16, so she is really broken.
>
> (Girl, aged 22)

For many children and young people who grow up in both kinship and non-kinship care, their relationship with their parents may involve disappointment, loss and ambivalent feelings – both during their childhood and in adult life. The stories of both Emilie (20) and Liv (25) illustrate this:

> For many years, my mum was so deep into drugs that I wasn't allowed to see her. She sent me birthday and Christmas presents. Of course it was really sad, because my friends celebrated their birthdays with their mums, while mine just sent presents in the post
>
> (Emilie, aged 20)

> She didn't call me on my birthday or anything. So the last time I saw her I said to her "you do realise that it was your daughter's birthday last week?". "Oh, Christ, I forgot" – like it was some sort of excuse, and ... "I wasn't well", and lots of stuff like that. I suppose I'm thinking that a mother who gives birth to a child does not forget the birthday, really. I don't really mind about that, but I do find it a bit frustrating, yet another confirmation of how little I have meant to her, really.
>
> (Liv, aged 25)

Some may also experience different forms of shame or embarrassment because of their parents' neglect or life situation. In the interviews where this was mentioned, shame or embarrassment was usually context-dependent – for example, a concrete situation where the mother's life situation became visible to others:

> Yes, I do remember meeting her on the bus when she was really out of it. She loves me very much, she really, really loves me – so she

would begin shouting on the bus, like: My daughter! And that was of course very uncomfortable. But in situations like that I usually ran away and hid, so that she wouldn't see me (laughs).

(Girl, aged 22)

Despite the fact that irritation, disappointment and several other negative feelings were often raised in the interviews with teenagers and young adults, very few had cut off contact with their parents. However, that does not mean that some hadn't toyed with the idea, people like Nora (aged 26):

The thought has crossed my mind, and it was the last thing we talked about, that I really can't be doing with this anymore. But it just never seems to happen, in a way. There is always another "I really can't be doing with this" (laughs a little).

That many children continue to have their parents in their lives in different ways and to different extents as adults is a feature of our data which can be interpreted in several ways. For some it may be the case that their parents' lives have significantly improved over time. Where this is not the case, on the other hand, contact with the parents can be understood as a form of generosity on the part of the young adults – they have reasons to break off contact, but most do not do it. However it can also illustrate a form of compulsion in the sense that the young adults, in line with social conventions, feel it to be almost impossible to break off the contact. Another interpretation is that many experience the presence of their parents as meaningful and rewarding despite the challenges the relationships may involve.

Conclusion

In the first part of this chapter we described the changed understandings of family and parenthood/parenting from the 1950s to the present day. Recent perspectives showing variation, fluidity and realities in family life and relationships have gained a great deal of influence in family research. Today there is extensive research literature illustrating the diversity of family forms and relationships in contemporary societies.

As emphasised in the second part of this chapter, variation is a common key word also in kinship foster families. Kinship foster families may resemble nuclear families with adopted children, non-kinship foster families or divorced and new, compound families. The childhood of children in kinship care can, for example, resemble the childhood of children whose parents are divorced in that they do not live with both parents. Different family types and relationships involve different experiences of growing up in kinship care. However, kinship care can also imply many similar experiences. Children who grow up with relatives appear to have more contact with the mother and her family than with the father and his family. There is also a predominance of women in the families that take care of the children. It is therefore true to say that many who grow up in kinship care experience a traditional pattern of gender roles as far as the care and responsibility of children are concerned. One question which should be asked in this context is whether, through their types of intervention, the CWS unintentionally contribute to maintaining these gender roles.

In this chapter we have particularly stressed the experiences of teenagers and young adults growing up in kinship care, that is, how they themselves present their upbringing/childhood and family. As we have seen, normality is a key word in these interviews. We do not know whether future children who grow up in kinship care also will emphasise normality. Since the CWS now have a legal obligation to look for foster care in families and networks it is possible that future children to a greater extent will grow up with relatives they do not know very well, and that kinship care will become more like non-kinship care. Future research will therefore to a greater extent have to investigate which factors promote, or prevent, understandings of normality in the lives of children and young people.

The experience of normality is not synonymous with the absence of challenges in childhood. As shown in this chapter, several of the teenagers and young adults related such challenges to the life situation of their parents. Many had experienced disappointment when their expectations of the parents, especially the mothers, had not been met. With a basis in theories of individualisation, one may wonder why the children, as adults, do not break off contact with their parents more often. In one of our articles we showed that it can be very difficult, if not impossible to break off contact, also when it is an expressed wish (Skoglund, Thørnblad & Holtan, 2018). Even if they have no contact with the parents, they cannot move away from the relationship. It nevertheless seems that many teenagers and young adults actually want to have their parents in their lives, even if their presence has involved, and still does involve, challenges. In our view these examples are contrary to theories of individualisation.

The relationships that children have with their parents are as varied as families in general. As we have shown, the language for describing variations in family structures or relationships is limited in this context. What do you call a mother who is not regarded as a mother, but more like a sister or a girlfriend, or when the mother's position is occupied by an aunt? The language used for family structures and relationships describes traditional family ideals where the nuclear family and biology are the norm. The traditional terms used for the categories nuclear family, stepfamily and foster family have little room for the variations in relationships and role descriptions of family members in the differentiated family picture of which kinship care is a part. As we have seen, the lack of alternatives "forces" us to use foster care terminology because the linguistic repertoire has not been sufficiently developed to reflect the variation in family structures and relationships.

Notes

1 The Parsonian image of the transition from the extended to the nuclear family as a result of the industrial revolution has been challenged. Kari Wærness (1976), for example, claimed that nuclear families existed in Norway before the process of industrialisation.
2 In 2016 the average age of moving in for the first time was 5.5 years for those living in foster care (Official Report NOU 2018: 18, 2018, pp. 51–52). The figures for calculating the average age were specially commissioned from the child welfare data (Statistics Norway) by the Foster Care Committee in connection with work on the report "Safe frameworks for foster care". The report was delivered to the Ministry of Children and Equality in December 2018.
3 The purpose of supervision is to oversee whether the child receives proper care in the foster home, and that the presupposed conditions for the placements are followed up (Section 4–22, Child Welfare Act).

References

Beck, U., & Beck-Gernsheim, E. (1995). *The normal chaos of love*. Cambridge, England: Polity Press.
Beck, U., & Beck-Gernsheim, E. (2002). *Individualization: Institutionalized individualism and its social and political consequences*. London, England: Sage.
Brandth, B., & Kvande, E. (2003). *Fleksible fedre. Maskulinitet, arbeid, velferdsstat*. Oslo, Norway: Universitetsforlaget.
Burgess, C., Rossvoll, F., Wallace, B., & Daniel, B. (2010). 'It's just like another home, just another family, so it's nae different' children's voices in kinship care: A research study about the experience of children in

kinship care in Scotland. *Child and Family Social Work, 15*(3), 297–306. doi:10.1111/j.1365-2206.2009.00671.x.

Egelund, T., Jakobsen, T. B., & Steen, L. (2010). *"Det er jo min familie!" Beretninger fra børn og unge i slægtspleje.* (Rapport nr. 10:34). København, Denmark: SFI.

Finch, J. (2007): Displaying families. *Sociology, 41*(1), 65–81. doi:10.1177/0038038507072284.

Forsberg, L. (2010). Engagerat föräldraskap som norm och praktik. *Sosiologi i dag, 40*(1–2), 78–98.

Giddens, A. (1992). *The transformation of intimacy: Sexuality, love and eroticism in modern societies.* Cambridge, England: Polity Press.

Gilding, M. (2010). Reflexivity over and above convention: The new orthodoxy in the sociology of personal life, formerly sociology of the family. *The British Journal of Sociology, 61*(4), 757–777.

Grue, L. (2016). *Normalitet.* Bergen, Norway: Fagbokforlaget.

Halldén, G. (1992). *Föräldrars tankar om barn. Uppfostringsideologi som kultur.* Stockholm: Carlsson Bokförlag.

Hays, S. (1996). *The cultural contradictions of motherhood.* New Haven, CT: Yale University Press.

Holtan, A. (2002). *Barndom i fosterhjem i egen slekt.* (Doktoravhandling). Universitetet i Tromsø.

Holtan, A. (2008). Family types and social integration in kinship foster care. *Children and Youth Services Review, 30*(9), 1022–1036. doi:10.1016/j.childyouth.2008.01.002.

Haavind, H. (2006). Midt i tredje akt? Fedres deltakelse i det omsorgsfulle foreldreskap. *Tidsskrift for Norsk psykologforening, 43*(7), 683–693.

Kitterød, R. H., & Rønsen, M. (2013). *Yrkes- og familiearbeid i barnefasen. Endring og variasjon i foreldres tidsbruk 1970–2010.* (Rappporter 44/2013). Oslo-Kongsvinger: Statistisk sentralbyrå.

Levin, I. (2004). Living apart together: A new family form. *Current Sociology, 52*(2), 223–240. doi:10.1177/0011392104041809.

Morgan, D. (1996). *Family connections: an introduction to family studies.* Cambridge, England: Polity Press.

Morgan, D. (1999). Risk and family practices: Accounting for change and fluidity in family life. In E. Silva & C. Smart (Eds.), *The new family?* (pp. 13–30). London, England: Sage.

Morgan, D. (2011). Framing relationships and families. In L. Jamieson, R. Simpson, & R. Lewis (Eds.), *Researching families and relationships* (pp. 19–30). Basingstoke, UK: Palgrave Macmillan.

Parsons, T. (1955). The American family: Its relations to personality and to the social structure. In T. Parsons & B. F. Bales (Eds.), *Family, socialization and interaction process* (pp. 3–33). Glencoe, IL: The Free Press.

Parsons, T., & Bales, R. F. (1955). *Family, socialization and interaction process.* Glencoe, IL: The Free Press.

Plantin, L. (2001). *Män, familjeliv og föräldraskap.* Umeå: Boréa Bokförlag.

Skoglund, J., Thørnblad, R., & Holtan, A. (2018). Children's relationships with birth parents in childhood and adulthood: A qualitative longitudinal study of kinship care. *Qualitative Social Work, 18*(6), 944–964. doi:10.1177/1473325018784646.

Solvang, P. (2006). Problematisering, utdefinering eller omfavnelse? Om normalitet. In T. Hylland Eriksen & J.-K. Breivik (Eds.), *Normalitet* (pp. 167–186). Oslo: Universitetsforlaget.

Stefansen, K. (2011). *Foreldreskap i småbarnsfamilien: Klassekultur og sosial reproduksjon*. (Doktoravhandling). Universitetet i Oslo.

Stern, D. N. (1985). *The interpersonal world of the infant: A view from psychoanalysis and developmental psychology*. New York, NY: Basic Books.

Storhaug, A. S. (2015). *Barnevernets forståelse av farskap*. (Doktoravhandling). Norges teknisk-naturvitskapelige universitet (NTNU).

Storhaug, A. S., Kojan, B. H., & Kvaran, I. (2012). Enslige mødre i kontakt med barnevernet. *Fontene forskning, 12*(2), 4–17.

Syltevik, L. J. (2000). *Differensierte familieliv: Familiepraksis i Norge på slutten av 1990-tallet*. (SEFOS Rapport nr. 2/2000). Bergen: Senter for samfunnsforskning, Universitetet i Bergen.

Thørnblad, R., & Holtan, A. (2011). Oppvekst i slektsfosterhjem: unge voksne fosterbarns familieforståelser. *Tidsskrift for undomsforskning, 11*(1), 49–67.

Warhuus Smeby, K. (2017). *Likestilling i det tredje skiftet? Heltidsarbeidende småbarnsforeldres praktisering av familieansvar etter 10 uker med fedrekvote*. (Doktoravhandling). Norges teknisk-naturvitenskapelige universitet (NTNU).

Wærness, K. (1976). Familien. In E. Øyen (Ed.), *Sosiologi og ulikhet* (pp. 48–61). Oslo, Norway: Universitetsforlaget.

7   Conclusion

Kinship care today and in the future

Changes in kinship care

The families who participated in our study when it started at the end of the 1990s had become foster parents at a time when kinship care was synonymous with risk. Many grandparents had been rejected as foster homes by the CWS at the time of the official care order. It is reasonable to assume that stories like the one about a grandmother's battle with the children's services (Chapter 5) are less prevalent today.

However, it is not only social and political guidelines for kinship care which have changed since the start of our research project. During the past 20 years there have also been changes in how family life in general is understood and practised. The position of children has been strengthened, and there is a far greater expectation that fathers should be involved in the interaction with and care of children. In line with these changes the understandings and practice of the CWS have changed as well; children have, for example, been given the rights and greater possibilities to influence decisions made by the CWS in cases that concern them. Changes in kinship care must be understood in relation to such general societal changes.

Changes in kinship care can also be linked to new recruitment practices in the CWS. As described in the introduction, a large number of families in our project were self-recruited. This means that the relatives themselves took the initiative to assume the care of a particular child rather than signalling a general interest in becoming foster parents. The CWS had only taken the initiative in a kinship care placement for one in five children. Local authorities now have a legal obligation to *search* for placement opportunities in the child's family and network. It is therefore safe to assume that more kinship foster parents are now being recruited "from outside" by CWS. This has probably provided, and will continue to provide, greater variation in family relationships.

DOI: 10.4324/9781003231363-7

The category 'kinship care' is likely to be more heterogenous now than what was the case for our data, where the majority of foster parents were grandmothers and others with close, established relationships with the child. Current recruitment practices involve new and different ways of working and new questions for research.

We do not know the answer to the question of how different kinship care is today compared to 20 years ago, nor what any of the possible changes involve. Features of the development may result in new and different challenges in the work of the CWS and give researchers different issues to investigate. However, even if future research may show more varied family constellations, relationships and practices, it will not necessarily reflect anything completely new. This argument is supported in particular by family sociological research contributions which show that family has changed, but has in no way been replaced by alternatives (Syltevik, 2018)

Kinship care, unintended consequences and the need for new questions

Given that kinship care has been prioritised by the CWS as an intervention since the last millennium, it is time to focus our attention on the possible unintended consequences of placing kin on the same level as foster families in the child welfare system. Our studies indicate that many children grow up in well-functioning kinship care families. One possible unintended consequence may be that these children end up with unnecessarily long client careers in the children's services due to equal judicial regulations.

Children who grow up with grandparents or others in their family and network have had a life situation which comes under what can be regarded as the most serious CWS area of responsibility, often called "core child protection". Later on, when the children's situation has improved, the work of the CWS is more about securing satisfactory conditions for the child to grow up in. The question that needs to be asked is whether it is "in the best interest" of the children that those who grow up with relatives with the resources to continue to provide good care remain clients of the CWS over time. However, the argument in favour of a greater degree of "discharge" from the CWS must not be confused with a wish for further privatisation of society's responsibility for children who need someone other than their parents to look after them. The welfare state's contribution to economic support for this group of children and families could be secured without the need for a client relationship with the CWS.

Our studies yielded a number of examples of relatives who had been responsible for caring for a child from an early age and who later found this responsibility formalised through an official care order and the signing of a foster care agreement. Such agreements can last until the child is an adult regardless of how the case has developed. For individuals and their families this implies contact with the children's services for up to 18 years – and even longer in the case of agreed follow-up care. Here we need to ask if this is *always* the best way to safeguard the interests of the child. If a child can grow up with relatives or others in their social network, does it have to be as a foster care arrangement and therefore made a part of the responsibility and control system of the children's services?

On the flip side there are examples of unfortunate unintended consequences of a too strong belief in the capacities of kinship care, or a presumption that kinship in itself can compensate for any shortcomings. Foster care regulations provide comprehensive rules for the approval of foster homes, and it is emphasised that the individuals who are chosen must have a "particular ability to provide a safe home for the child". At the same time it is possible to deviate somewhat from certain rules if it undoubtedly is in the best interests of the child to be placed in their family and network (Official Report NOU 2018: 18, 2018, p. 40). If the importance of a kinship relationship is over-emphasised at the expense of other qualities, this may have unfortunate consequences for the child. It can also mean that the control apparatus which regulates all foster care is toned down or gets side-lined in cases where it is legitimate, and as a consequence children and families would not get the help they need and the child remains in a vulnerable situation.

In other words, kinship care poses challenges for the CWS. In interviews with case workers, several state that working with kinship care is different from working with non-kinship care, and that it requires different kinds of understandings (Dimmen & Trædal, 2013). The authors argue that the difference lies in the familial relationships, the obligations and the emotional qualities – conditions which otherwise are considered to be the strength of kinship care. The case workers felt that this difference had the potential to limit the scope for action by the CWS in these families compared with non-kinship care. As we see it, it is reasonable to assume that the challenges faced by the case workers are linked to the uncertainty about what kinship care really *is* and what it should be treated as. To an even greater extent than with non-kinship care, kinship care finds itself in the intersection between the private and the public sphere. It is therefore not at all obvious which strategies for action must or should apply (cf. Table 4.1).

Current child welfare policy and legislation strongly prioritises kinship and networks. However, it is not at all certain what kinship care will look like in the future. Put simply, we envisage two directions. First, a development towards the standardisation of foster care, i.e. with increased specialisation of the foster parent role and general professionalisation. Second, a development which to a greater extent builds on an understanding of family, where official frameworks, assistance and control are harmonised with what is applicable for other compound family constellations in our society. Given that the kinship foster families do, and increasingly will, constitute a heterogeneous group in the future, there will most probably be a need for both – both for children to grow up in kinship care under the control and guidance of the CWS, and with relatives as a private family affair. In Norway today, we do not have regulations and facilitation which allow families who wish to care for the children of relatives to do so without the lasting involvement of the CWS.

Research on kinship care – gaps in knowledge

The extended use of kinship care and a possible development towards a more diverse group of kinship foster parents open up for new research questions. There is a need for updated research on what characterises kinship care today. So far there has been little research across the Nordic and other European countries in this field. The establishment of research networks across national borders might contribute to the widening of research-based knowledge in this area.

As described in Chapter 3, research that has been carried out up to the present day has been dominated by studies attempting to discover the effects of kinship care, often compared with non-kinship care. The studies have in a broad sense investigated the use of kinship care along the continuum between the perspectives of risk and resources. Examples of this include what kind of impact kinship care has on placement stability, the child's behaviour, mental health and school performance.

Some issues in the research on kinship care as an intervention remain unanswered or not sufficiently investigated. This is particularly true of studies based on the heterogeneity in the kinship care category. Questions could, for example, be asked about *what* in kinship care gives good and less good outcomes. Such issues would benefit from a mixed methods research design which combines quantitative data on outcomes with qualitative studies on understandings. Such studies would give the CWS knowledge of what is required in order for kinship care to result in the desired outcomes, but also of the type of support which is needed by the various families according to the challenges they may face. Studies like these would be useful for the development of future policies which prepare the groundwork for both kinship care under the control of the children's services and for growing up with relatives as a private agreement.

There is also a need for research into growing up with relatives from perspectives that are not based on the definitions of the CWS, but which open the paths to topics and issues that are different to those usually dealt with by the intervention research. One area which deserves attention is the impact of long-term state regulation and support in kinship care – how the frameworks and involvement of the CWS affect the lives of the children and adults, and their understanding of childhood, parenting roles and family. Another practically non-investigated topic is kinship care (and non-kinship care) in a gender perspective. Kinship care as a phenomenon is characterised by a pattern of traditional gender roles (cf. Chapter 5). It is usually women who assume the responsibility for other relative's children, often as replacements for the child's mother. This does not mean that men are not care providers, but the pattern is for women to carry out the main responsibility. The consequences of this for women from the perspective of equality, for example, whether carrying out the tasks of a caregiver affects their working life and financial independence, have not been studied. Research results from various theoretical, methodological and thematic perspectives will provide useful knowledge in the development of new possible solutions for growing up in kinship care, both inside and outside the CWS system. On a system level it would also be appropriate to investigate the degree to which research results are used by authorities and child welfare workers.

The CWS codify understandings and categorisations which guide the work of the system – while other ways of understanding gain less attention. Different types of families are adapted and redefined to fit the categories that are available in the system. We would like to stress the importance, both for the development of practice and for research, of bringing to light the variation in the life situations of children and families who today find themselves in the category kinship care. Our point here is that the categories currently available in the CWS system do not sufficiently take into account the variations which we have described in this book. This requires new legislation and terminology which reflect variations.

References

Dimmen, S. A., & Trædal, F. (2013). Fosterhjemsplassering i slekt og nettverk – Handlingsrom og dilemmaer. *Tidsskriftet Norges Barnevern, 90*(3), 158–173.

NOU 2018: 18. (2018). *Trygge rammer for fosterhjem.* Oslo, Norway: Barne- og likestillingsdepartementet.

Syltevik, L. J. (2018). A sociological perspective on changes in the family in Norway. In T. Tilden & B. E. Wampold (Eds.), *Routine outcome monitoring in couple and family therapy* (pp. 45–62). (E-bok). Cham, Sveits: Springer Nature.

Index

kinship families 5–6; *see also* family/ies
kinship foster care 1; *see also* kinship care
kinship foster homes 68, 73, 89–91; *see also* foster care
kinship foster parents 77–92; examples of background to agreement to foster 79–82; grandmothers 85–87; grandparents as foster parents 84–85; kinship care and women 82–83; kinship care as class phenomenon 89–91; and matrilineal kinship 83–84; personal care 87–89
Kvande, E. 101

Larsen, G. 34

Mason, J. 78
matrilineal kinship 83–84
matrilinear kinship 84
mental health: of children in kinship care 41–42; of children in non-kinship care 41–42; measurement 43
Moldestad, B. 29
Moller, Christen C. 19–20
monopolising family 103
Morgan, David 96–97
mothers: grandmothers in role of 85–87; inadequate 108–111; single 83
multi-nuclear family 103; *see also* family/ies

negotiations: and CWS 62; defined 78; on responsibility 78–79
network, defined 5–6
"The New Child Welfare Services" project 83
New Public Management 13
non-kinship care 1, 10, 30; mental health of children in 41–42; and permanency 44
non-kinship foster homes 88, 90
normality, and family understanding 104–106
Norwegian Child Welfare Act 77
Norwegian Directorate for Children, Youth and Family Affairs 35n5

Norwegian Life Course, Ageing and Generation Study (NorLAG) 84–85, 92n3

Office for Children, Youth and Family Affairs (Bufetat) 60
"Outcomes and Experience of Foster Care" 3, 4, **4**

parenthood: changing patterns of 98–100; described 99
"Parenting Stress Index" 92n4
parents 99; contact with children in foster care 25–27; father as 100–101; visitation rights 25–27; *see also* family/ies; kinship foster parents
Parsons, Talcott 95–96, 101
permanency: and kinship care 44; and non-kinship care 44
personal care: different rationalities **58**; obligations and costs 87–89; and professional practice 57–60
placement: of children with relatives 27–29; defined 14; sites for children in care in Norway in 1947 **21**; *see also* foster care; kinship care
Plantin, L. 101
Poor Act (1863) 35n1
poor relief 13
practice: family as 96–97; professional 57–60; reflective 98
private lives, and child welfare services 66–68
"private sphere" 74n1
professional care: different rationalities **58**; and logic of the workplace 58; and specialist knowledge 58
professional practice 57–60
"public sphere" 74n1
pure relationship 98

randomised controlled trials (RCT) 45
reflective practices 98
relationship: of child to foster parents **84**; contractual 56–57; maintaining 98–99; pure 98
remuneration: financial 64–65; between support and reward 63–64

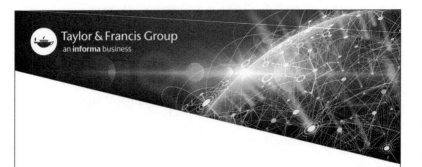

For Product Safety Concerns and Information please contact our EU representative GPSR@taylorandfrancis.com Taylor & Francis Verlag GmbH, Kaufingerstraße 24, 80331 München, Germany

Batch number: 08158401

Printed by Printforce, the Netherlands